D1325565

# A Decade of Manpower Development and Training

Garth L. Mangum
John Walsh

Olympus Publishing Company  Salt Lake City, Utah

# Contents

# List of Tables

# 1

# The MDTA Program in Retrospect

It has been said that social policy in the United States follows a systematic issue-attention cycle[1] which consists of (1) a preproblem stage wherein certain undesirable yet long-ignored social conditions develop, (2) a gradually penetrating awareness and then alarmed discovery that these conditions exist, with an attendant euphoric enthusiasm for workable solutions, (3) a slow realization of the prohibitive costs of these solutions, and finally (4) a waning of public interest, leaving behind a residue of activity maintained by those who manned programs that were instigated during the euphoric stage. This issue-attention cycle well describes the ten-year experience that the United States has sustained in its manpower policy, marked from its beginnings by the passage of the Manpower Development and Training Act (MDTA) in 1962.

The MDTA experience produces some variations on the issue-attention theme. Passage of the Act wedded an overdue concern for manpower planning for the long run with a misreading of the current problem. Since a fairly broad clientele had been selected for MDTA to serve, its first decade was marked by quiet bipartisan support. Meanwhile, other manpower programs were to some degree spawned as MDTA's children. These programs drew the heat of controversy as they focused on a narrower and less popular target group. Funds appropriated for MDTA were persistently drained away to finance whatever panacea

---

[1] Anthony Downs, "Up and Down with Ecology: The Issue-Attention Cycle," *The Public Interest*, no. 28 (Summer 1972).

74-07328

was most prevalent at the moment. In the meantime, fragmented evaluations gave MDTA clear marks for success, even as its objectives shifted to more difficult tasks.

In preparation for MDTA's tenth anniversary, a massive evaluation effort was initiated which could not only identify numerous administrative problems and needed reforms, but also provide generally supportive statistics. Yet that birthday arrived amid doubt that the Act would survive its decennial year. It narrowly survived, despite waning support and fragmenting bipartisanship, and then faced its eleventh birthday with its survival once again in doubt, for the first time with active opposition reinforcing the previous apathy.

It is the purpose of this book to evaluate the ten-year experience, less from attack or defense of a particular program than as an assessment of the economic and social role of an adult remedial skills training activity. The history of the origins and early experience under the Act has been told elsewhere.[2] It is necessary here only to review the conditions and premises from which it emerged and note the major policy changes which affected both its nature and its objectives. In succeeding chapters, we review and evaluate the Act's experience, while in the final chapter we draw conclusions and make recommendations from the evaluation.

## Objectives and Sources of MDTA

During the 1950s, the nation was beset by creeping unemployment. Late in that decade, congressional leaders, many of whom had lived through and all too vividly recalled the Great Depression of the 1930s, were quick to recognize the impending peril but slow to find a program to buttress the sagging labor market. Some supported a short-run program that would immediately start to rectify the condition, while others stressed a flexible, ongoing program that could be adapted to diverse locales and situations. To be truly effective, they all agreed, the program would have to take the short- and the long-run views.

### Short- and Long-Run Objectives

The force primarily responsible for the short-run projections and the passage of MDTA in 1962 was the aforementioned rising unemployment, coincidentally peaking at a critical time to affect the 1960

---

[2] Garth L. Mangum, *MDTA, Foundation of Federal Manpower Policy* (Baltimore: Johns Hopkins University Press, 1968).

national elections and then settling upon a high plateau. The entire campaign period was spent in arguing whether creeping unemployment in truth existed. The causes of the phenomenon were even less easy to agree upon. The popular explanations, each strongly held by various groups, were three: (1) technological change, classified as automation, was displacing experienced workers, leaving their skills obsolete and themselves stranded in the labor market; (2) structural changes, some of them from automation, were concentrating unemployment by age, race, sex, location, and education while so twisting labor market demand to leave jobs at higher levels unfilled; (3) the economy was simply not growing rapidly enough to absorb the swollen numbers of new entrants to the labor force and those normally displaced by rising productivity.

Those holding the first two views were convinced that no shortage of jobs existed . . . it was a case of square pegs unable to fill round holes. To reshape the pegs by means of retraining programs seemed a reasonable answer. Meanwhile, those holding the third view, anxious for any increase in total expenditures which would spark a revival of growth, could see nothing particularly wrong with spending for training. But — that was the short run.

The longer run interest was pushed by those who were convinced that the nation was undergoing a manpower revolution.[3] An economy which had largely expected manpower resources to adapt rather easily to the demands placed upon them as they combined with natural and capital resources in the production process would now have to give primacy to human resource considerations. Essentially, this interest was subdivided between a congressional concern for manpower planning and a U.S. Department of Labor (DOL) interest in manpower and labor market research. Senator Joseph S. Clark, the MDTA program's author in that branch of the legislature, envisioned as the ideal a "Council of Manpower Advisers," modeled after the Council of Economic Advisers, which could foresee the nation's manpower and employment needs and derive policies to achieve them. DOL statistics technicians wanted a broad charter for manpower research. All believed that manpower considerations deserved higher visibility in the total national policy-making process, and of course, they also believed in training for the unemployed. Those manpower planning and research ambitions are

---

[3] Garth L. Mangum, *The Manpower Revolution* (New York: Doubleday, 1965).

especially worth noting in relationship to subsequent experience and current interest.

## Designing a Program

It is one thing to write a charter but quite another to launch a program. Congress had to ask itself: Where is the capability to administer such a program? The initial explorations of Congress led in the direction of the U.S. Office of Education (USOE), but found no response. DOL on the other hand responded with enthusiasm, derived its own bill, and won presidential approval of it. Education associations saved a role for USOE, but the early disinterest left it no more than a junior partnership.

Administration at the state and local levels was never in doubt. There were only two agencies available — the public schools and the public employment services (ES) — each a semi-independent recipient of federal funds. The federal-state ES partnership consisted of full federal funding and considerable influence over 2,000 nominally state-operated ES offices whose primary functions were administering unemployment compensation and referring applicants in response to employer job orders. USOE provided modest matching funds but exercised little influence over vocational education activities in the states. ES and vocational education together provided a ready combination of vehicles to launch a remedial skills training program. ES could identify eligible people (primarily experienced but unemployed adults) and occupations offering "reasonable expectation of employment" after training. It could then request the public schools to mount skills training for those occupations, could pay stipends to the trainees closely equal to what they would expect to receive from unemployment compensation, and could then refer them to jobs when their training was completed.

On-the-job training (OJT), financed by reimbursement to employees for training expenses, was expected to be a parallel effort. However, institutional training, as the school version came to be known, had a built-in local administering bureaucracy which did not exist for OJT, leaving the latter to a late start and a slow growth. The triple role of the federal government was two-agency approval of each project, funding through DOL appropriations, and DOL-sponsored research into the causes of unemployment and other manpower problems.

*Shifting Objectives*

It is necessary to the understanding of subsequent policy developments to recognize the differing philosophy and structure of DOL and USOE relative to manpower programs in general and MDTA in particular. To DOL administrators, a job has typically been both the end and the means in manpower policy. With a foot on a career ladder, ideally the trainees were to find that wages would take care of personal problems and employers would take care of training needs. To USOE, education has been both means and end. Sufficient training was to prepare the enrollees for present jobs and future adaptability.

DOL aggressively sought the assignment to administer other manpower programs, as well as MDTA, and soon found 80 percent of its budget emanating from manpower sources, with an assistant secretary and most of its employees engaged in those activities. MDTA, assigned to the fifth tier in the U.S. Department of Health, Education and Welfare (HEW) hierarchy under the low-prestige vocational education bureau, was given only a handful of staff to supervise the actual training function, and thus no companion manpower programs were sought by or given to HEW. Consequently, the primary voice in MDTA policy was DOL, with the tiny USOE-MDTA staff fighting a rear guard action, often with unbureaucratically subversive weapons to influence policy in their direction.

Following the MDTA program's initiation, a bipartisan coalition was formed which continually extended and broadened its authority as requested by the Administration; in fact, congressmen frequently went beyond Administration requests in broadening the program's scope, if not its funding. Stipends were increased, authorized training duration was lengthened, youth were given a larger share of the training resources and emphasis, basic education and communications skills were endorsed, relocation assistance was experimented with, professionals were allowed refurbishing, experiment and demonstration were added to research, prerelease training for prisoners was allowed, and so forth.

The most important shift in objectives was made administratively rather than through legislative amendment, but was subsequently endorsed by Congress. Following President Johnson's declaration of a "war on poverty," the program trended toward inclusion of a more disadvantaged clientele, especially in the institutional training component through the introduction of "Skills Centers" specially developed to serve that group. In 1966, the objective was explicitly declared to be 65 percent of the training for the disadvantaged with 35 percent to be used to alleviate labor shortages, the latter being of concern to businessmen in the tightening labor markets of 1966 and 1967. Since no one could objectively measure service to the disadvantaged without a definition of that term, it was classified in early 1968 as "those who are both poor and without satisfactory employment" plus one of the following:

Under 21 or over 44 years of age

Having less than a high school education

Being a member of a minority group

Being physically or mentally handicapped

MDTA was now an antipoverty program to be judged by its ability to contribute to that objective.

*Diversion of MDTA Funds*

It was in pursuit of this antipoverty objective that DOL thrust out in a number of directions searching for a job-oriented alternative more effective than institutional training. Since Congress had legislated only MDTA and the Economic Opportunity Act (EOA) — plus the 1967 beginning of punitive Social Security legislation aimed at reducing welfare roles — and DOL was not prepared to seek new legislation, the funds for what came to be known as "panacea hopping" had to be drained from the existing programs. HEW meanwhile maintained its faith in institutional training, but experimented to adapt it to the needs of the disadvantaged.

DOL sought to expand the OJT component, but found employers more likely to seek reimbursement for training the nondisadvantaged. Alarmed at the growing restiveness in ghetto areas, especially after the Watts riot in Los Angeles, the Secretary of Labor directed a reallocation of funding to concentrate expenditures and services in the most poverty-stricken central city census tracts. The Concentrated Employment Program (CEP) was launched without congressional authorization (though subsequently endorsed by appropriations committees) and financed in part with funds which would otherwise have gone into institutional training.

The original hope of CEP was that given a persistently rising demand for labor, and with minor rejuvenation of disadvantaged enrollees, private employers could be convinced to place the disadvantaged on their payrolls. When this hope was thwarted, a series of experimental projects began, leading to the initiation of the National Alliance of Businessmen and its Job Opportunities in the Business Sector (NAB-JOBS) program in 1968, again funded in part from MDTA appropriation. Public Service Careers (PSC) was added as a public counterpart to encourage employment of disadvantaged persons in public agencies. The Cooperative Area Manpower Planning System (CAMPS) was also financed primarily with MDTA funds.

In the meantime, HEW faced reductions in enrollment at the Skills Centers it had encouraged state vocational educators to undertake for the training of the disadvantaged. Launched on the upswing of appropriations and with expenditure delays which accumulated funds from previous fiscal years, these institutions were able to begin at spending rates not supportable over the long run. But the diversion of MDTA funds to CEP, PSC, CAMPS, and other efforts reduced the period over which high enrollment could have been supported (see Table 1-1). Monies obligated to actual institutional training moved rapidly upward to a peak of $254 million between 1963 and 1965, then slumped and did not reach or supersede that peak again until 1970. Total MDTA obligations in 1971 were more than double those of 1966, whereas expenditures on institutional training were up only 9 percent. Enrollments followed the pattern similar to that of the finances.

In a sense, such EOA manpower programs as the Neighborhood Youth Corps (NYC), Job Corps, Operation Mainstream, and New Careers were also a diversion of funds from MDTA. MDTA's original charter was broad and Congress had shown a readiness to amend it upon request. There is nothing in the manpower components of EOA which could not have been added to MDTA. The motivations for separate acts and programs were several; first, probably most important, was the distrust with which the antipoverty program designers viewed ES and the vocational schools. Those established institutions had not, would not, and probably could not serve the poor, it was charged. In fact, the antipoverty warriors sought to bypass most established institutions, including state and local governments, in favor of newly created ad hoc

## Table 1-1

## Manpower Development and Training Activities
### Cumulative Obligations[a] by Agency and Program
(Millions of dollars)

| Category | Fiscal Year | | | | | | | | | Total All Years |
|---|---|---|---|---|---|---|---|---|---|---|
| | 1963 | 1964 | 1965 | 1966 | 1967 | 1968 | 1969 | 1970 | 1971 | |
| Total MDTA obligations | $66.6 | $120.0 | $354.1 | $354.2 | $355.0 | $386.4 | $398.0 | $697.2 | $791.7 | $3,520.2[b] |
| DOL | 36.8 | 51.2 | 240.8 | 230.4 | 257.6 | 260.6 | 277.5 | 535.9 | 636.6 | 2,527.4 |
| HEW | 29.8 | 68.8 | 110.3 | 123.8 | 97.4 | 125.7 | 119.6 | 154.4 | 146.8 | 976.6 |
| Other agencies[c] | | | | | | 0.1 | 1.0 | 6.8 | 8.3 | 16.2 |
| Total federal salaries and expenses | 5.7 | 10.2 | 11.8 | 1.9 | 2.4 | 2.4 | 3.0 | 2.6 | | 40.0 |
| DOL | 5.0 | 9.2 | 10.4 | | 0.5 | 0.2 | 0.4 | | | 25.7 |
| HEW | 0.7 | 1.0 | 1.4 | 1.9 | 1.9 | 2.2 | 2.6 | 2.6 | | 14.3 |
| Total state admin. and program services | 6.5 | 10.4 | 34.3 | 32.2 | 37.1 | 44.9 | 51.0 | 90.1 | 94.3 | 400.8 |
| DOL — program services[d] | 5.6 | 8.8 | 30.2 | 24.8 | 32.5 | 36.9 | 43.0 | 79.6 | 83.7 | 345.1 |
| HEW — state admin. and support | 0.9 | 1.6 | 4.1 | 7.4 | 4.6 | 8.0 | 8.0 | 10.5 | 10.6 | 55.7 |
| Total direct program | 54.4 | 99.4 | 305.0 | 320.1 | 315.5 | 339.0 | 343.1 | 597.6 | 689.1 | 3,063.2 |
| DOL | 26.2 | 33.2 | 200.2 | 205.6 | 224.6 | 223.5 | 234.1 | 456.3 | 552.9 | 2,156.6 |
| HEW | 28.2 | 66.2 | 104.8 | 114.5 | 90.9 | 115.5 | 109.0 | 141.3 | 136.2 | 906.6 |
| Direct programs | | | | | | | | | | |
| Total institutional[e] | 51.0 | 86.4 | 254.0 | 251.5 | 204.0 | 219.1 | 214.1 | 287.1 | 276.3 | 1,843.5 |
| DOL | 22.8 | 20.2 | 149.2 | 141.0 | 120.8 | 113.7 | 114.2 | 165.8 | 155.3 | 1,003.0 |
| HEW | 28.2 | 66.2 | 104.8 | 110.5 | 83.2 | 105.4 | 99.9 | 121.3 | 121.0 | 840.5 |

| | | | | | | | | | | Total |
|---|---|---|---|---|---|---|---|---|---|---|
| Total on-the-job training | 3.4 | 11.2 | 29.0 | 46.3 | 73.6 | 53.4 | 56.5 | 49.5 | 61.4 | 384.3 |
| DOL | $ 3.4 | 11.2 | 29.0 | 45.0 | 68.2 | 44.7 | 52.4 | 44.1 | 58.0 | 356.0 |
| HEW | | | | 1.3 | 5.4 | 8.7 | 4.1 | 5.4 | 3.4 | 28.3 |
| JOBS — DOL (MDTAs) | | | | | 13.3 | 35.1 | 29.0 | 101.8 | 167.2 | 346.4 |
| Total PSC | | | | | | | | 36.0 | 13.3 | 49.3 |
| DOL | | | | | | | | 32.5 | 13.1 | 45.6 |
| HEW | | | | | | | | 3.5 | 0.2 | 3.7 |
| Total CEP | | | | 22.3 | 24.6 | 17.5 | 32.7 | 48.6 | 56.4 | 202.1 |
| DOL[f] | | | | 19.6 | 22.3 | 16.1 | 27.7 | 37.5 | 44.8 | 168.0 |
| HEW[g] | | | | $ 2.7 | $ 2.3 | 1.4 | 5.0 | 11.1 | 11.6 | 34.1 |
| Summer program — DOL | | | | | | 11.8 | 7.5 | $ 74.6 | $114.5 | 208.4 |
| All other — DOL | | $ 1.8 | $ 22.0 | | | | | $ 2.1 | $ 3.3 | $ 29.2 |
| Total enrollments[h] | 34.1 | 77.6 | 156.9 | 235.8 | 265.0 | 241.0 | 220.0 | 221.0 | 254.8 | 1,706.2 |
| Institutional | 32.0 | 68.6 | 145.3 | 177.5 | 150.0 | 140.0 | 135.0 | 130.0 | 155.6 | 1,134.0 |
| OJT | 2.1 | 9.0 | 11.6 | 58.3 | 115.0 | 101.0 | 85.0 | 91.0 | 99.2 | 572.2 |

[a] Cumulative obligations are the total of cumulative expenditures and certified unpaid obligations as of June 30, 1971.

[b] Of the $3,765.4 million appropriated through fiscal year 1971, $3,520.2 million were obligated; $75.5 million were the unobligated balance; and $169.7 million had been reverted to the U.S. Department of the Treasury. The breakdown on obligations and activities is not available for 1972; however, total appropriations for fiscal years 1963–72 were $4.7 billion.

[c] Other agencies include Public Service Careers, on-the-job training, and summer programs conducted through the Office of Economic Opportunity, the U.S. Department of Housing and Urban Development, the U.S. Department of the Interior-Environmental Protection Agency, and the U.S. Department of Justice.

[d] Program services include employment service administration, Cooperative Area Manpower Planning System, Job Bank, labor market information, and technical assistance.

[e] Total institutional includes part time and other.

[f] Concentrated Employment Program allowances and contracted training.

[g] Concentrated Employment Program in-house institutional training.

[h] Thousands of people.

community institutions more sympathetic toward and representative of the poor. Second, the notion of a war on poverty had captured some public and congressional imagination which could be exploited. Finally, new departures and new programs carry the names of and give political mileage to different politicians from those rewarded for the amendment of existing programs.

It was that fracturing of manpower policy out of the single program framework, along with what the states considered arbitrary DOL decisions, which led to the introduction of CAMPS as another MDTA-funded activity. Coordination of the many programs, all operating in the same areas and for essentially the same clients, became an issue. In addition, several states complained to their congressional delegations about national DOL decisions which limited their prerogative to make their own decisions. For instance, the institutional-OJT mix prescribed for each state by DOL, and the latter's practice of reallocating to other states those allocations not obligated early in a fiscal year, became a matter of contention. Out of this issue grew CAMPS, designed to bring into a joint planning activity all state and local agencies involved in the administration of federally funded manpower programs.

From this experience emerged the issues of "decategorization" and "decentralization." Categorical programs, it was argued, require those in need of manpower services to fit themselves to the eligibility rules and service availability of particular programs, rather than having available sources tailored to their needs. Localities had equally differing needs. However, CAMPS participants were never given sufficient discretion (in the use of the manpower funds allocated to them) to make manpower planning meaningful. Discretion to implement plans, a framework within which to plan, and training in how to plan — all seem necessary to make an attractive idea real.

## A DECLINING CONSENSUS

The decategorization-decentralization issue had been highlighted and argued sufficiently for the new Administration to adopt it as a priority manpower program reform in 1969. However, subsequent congressional reluctance to give up the political advantages of separate categories of programs, the Administration's unwillingness at one point to accept a public service employment component as the price of such a

bill's passage, the Administration's subsequent endorsement of an un-
acceptable (because it was excessive) form of decentralization, dissipa-
tion of the bipartisan manpower coalition, and growing disinterest in the
whole issue have blocked passage of any reform for four years . . . all of
which completes the circle, returning the onus to MDTA.

The MDTA program was slated to expire on June 30, 1971; however, congressional supporters of manpower administrative reforms
began "playing chicken" with an extension. Rather than see the training program expire, perhaps its supporters would pressure Congress to
pass a reform bill authorizing manpower training within the decate-
gorized authority. Because skills training is a process that encompasses
considerable lead time and extends over an average enrollment period of
approximately 30 weeks, facilities must be scheduled, instructors re-
tained, and expiration dates considered before training is begun. When
it became apparent in the spring of 1972 (coincidentally around the
tenth anniversary) that the program was winding down, supporters of
the reform bills (there are a number of them, all with similar interest)
in both DOL and Congress relented, and a one-year extension was
granted. The respite was brief, however, and by the beginning of 1973,
the entire process was again being threatened.

But this time there was a difference — a growing disillusion with
the results of all the social reforms undertaken during the previous
decade was being manifested throughout the land. None of the problems had disappeared or even been noticeably reduced, despite the investment in time, effort, and funds. Many liberals who had been architects of the programs during the previous Administration were now
recanting. They felt that the strategy of introducing programs to change
people and institutions was a failure and that income redistribution was
the answer. Besides, they told themselves, maybe the problems were not
as serious as they at first believed.

In an election year, recipients of the programs had not been among
those likely to vote for the Administration in power. Those who were in
control were critical of the expenditures on behalf of those for whom
they had no special affection. And persistently large budget deficits were
threatening, requiring either expenditure reduction or increased taxes.
Added to this fact was the evidence that success was limited for any of

the several social welfare programs; therefore this was an unpropitious time for any manpower program to face expiration.

The foregoing political factors are but coincidental to the motivation to publish this book. After a number of evaluations of various aspects of MDTA were completed, most of which we participated in, we determined to commit these data to paper. Thus a summary of the results of these evaluation will, hopefully, make them more available to the manpower fraternity. If legislative and administrative decisions are affected by our conclusions and recommendations, so much the better.

# 2

# The Outcomes of MDTA Training

After ten years of experience and a total of $4.7 billion in appropriations, the critical issue to consider about the future of MDTA lies in its past. Has the effort been worth the struggle? Have the benefits brought to society been greater than the costs imposed on that society? There is no simple answer . . . for an answer must depend first upon those factors which we consider benefits and those which we deem costly. Second, the answer depends upon finding a way to measure and compare benefits and costs.

Evaluations of manpower programs range from administrative evaluations (how well the program is being administered and how its functioning can be improved) to outcome studies (what has happened to the employment and earnings of the enrollees) to impact evaluations (what the impacts were on nonparticipants, communities, labor markets, and so forth). The choice of evaluation methods is in part a matter of expedience: What level of evaluation can be accomplished with the time and resources available? It is also a matter of objectives: What did the program seek to accomplish?

Though it was initially devised in straightforward terms that spelled out the route the program was to follow to reach definite goals, MDTA has been subject to as much confusion over objectives as any other social program. The criticism leveled at manpower training programs by a high official of the U.S. Department of the Treasury is an example.

He feels that such programs are a waste of money because they "haven't reduced the unemployment rate by as much as one-half of one percent!"

But who expected manpower training to reduce general levels of unemployment? That could be achieved only by (1) speeding the rate of economic growth and job creation, (2) adding to the efficiency of the labor market to reduce the average duration of unemployment, or (3) reducing the size of the labor force. A training program does none of these. It creates jobs only for training staffs. Conceivably, it could fill job vacancies; but there is no evidence that substantial numbers of job vacancies exist in occupations within the reach of MDTA. A training project might serve a placement role by increasing the visibility of the applicant. It might also take unemployed individuals from the labor market to receive training (that is, if enrollees were defined as out of the labor force). One might well be surprised if MDTA has in truth reduced the unemployment rate by as much as 0.5 percent.

Is there justification for expenditures of funds wrested from taxpayers in order to supply skills which can only increase competition for existing jobs? It is possible to argue that a better trained labor force might spark economic growth or might allow more growth with less inflation, but it is by no means certain or proved. The primary justification for manpower programs, including MDTA, rests upon a value judgment. The long-term objective of the American society has been the expansion of individual freedoms, achievable in a concrete sense only by broadening the range of choices available to each individual. If that can be accomplished by increasing the total supply of opportunity, so much the better. If not, each individual should have his choices expanded, even if by doing so, he forces others to face greater competition in attaining their choices. Thus, spreading the franchise dilutes the power of each vote; allowing new business enterprise may increase the competition faced by existing firms; encouraging collective bargaining adds constraints for the employers; and educating more people reduces the competitive edge of those already educated.

MDTA is best evaluated in this context. It would be well to know whether by training $A$, we make him capable of winning a job in preference to $B$ who would have otherwise obtained it. That would be one piece of an impact evaluation. But MDTA's role is a simple one: to identify individuals who, as defined by public policy, have limited opportunities and to expand those opportunities by training the individuals to enable them to compete more effectively for existing jobs. Demonstration of the program's ability to achieve these objectives requires only determination that most of those enrolled achieved improvements in their employment stability and earnings substantially beyond that which would have occurred in absence of the program. It is generally assumed that the benefits to the target population must exceed the costs to the remainder of society so that the total body of social welfare is enlarged. Since opporunity is difficult to measure in abstract terms, requiring income benefits to exceed resource costs is a useful defense against the tendency to use abstract and unmeasurable gains to justify programs not defensible through hard data.

MDTA is currently in the interesting posture of being defended by a mass of favorable but fragmentary and nondefinitive evidence offset by some meager defense for negative conclusions. The purpose of this chapter is to examine all available data on MDTA outcomes in search of some reasonable judgment as to the program's worth.

## The Weight of Scattered Studies

MDTA's worth remains unproved after a decade of experience, not because it has never been evaluated but because none of the existing evaluations — nor all of them in aggregate — have proved the program's worth beyond logical challenge. Until 1971, evaluations done by MDTA were scattered and fragmentary but generally consistent in their favorable results.

In evaluating the training component of the Area Redevelopment Act (ARA), a predecessor to MDTA, Gerald Somers and others[1] reported substantial initial income gains for the enrollee samples in comparison with control groups. The latter consisted of persons eligible for enrollment at the time but not seeking it, those selected for enrollment but not accepting it, and those who dropped out before they had completed the program. Obviously, completers may have differed in their attitudes if not their skills in comparison to the controls. Despite the favorable short-run results, these and later follow-up studies suggest that there is a tendency for the favorable margin (earnings of enrollees over

---

[1] Gerald G. Somers (ed.), *Retraining the Unemployed* (Madison: University of Wisconsin Press, 1968).

those of controls) of those who complete training to lessen with time. Nevertheless, as much as five years passed in some studies, with the margin, even though shrinking, still in favor of the completers.[2]

Connecticut and Massachusetts ARA studies also provide laudatory results, the Connecticut study showing persistent gains over five years.[3] Control groups were similarly constituted with the other studies. Hardin and Borus[4] also studied a limited enrollee sample in Michigan which was controlled by eligible persons who qualified for but did not seek training. The interesting conclusion was that enrollment in training programs paid off in incremental earnings, but once the trainee was enrolled, the shorter the time he remained in the program the better off he was. Training of less than 200 hours' duration paid off, but lengthier programs did not. One speculative possibility is that dropouts may have obtained jobs in a recovering auto industry while completers were being prepared for lower paid jobs, though the authors tended to discount that explanation.

The only significant nationwide follow-up study during the Act's first eight years examined 1,200 enrollees and a uniquely chosen control group of 925 who were asked to identify retrospectively their friends and relatives unemployed but not enrolled at the time of the program's beginnings. In addition, the researchers canvassed the neighborhoods for suitable control group members, leaving the nagging question of whether those who availed themselves of the opportunity to enroll could really be compared with those who did not. Nevertheless, the follow-up found substantial improvements in income, coming primarily from improved employment stability rather than higher wages.[5]

A large nationwide survey[6] examined the attitudes of former en-

---

[2] Gerald G. Somers and Graehme H. McKechnie, "Vocational Retraining Programs for the Unemployed," *Twentieth Annual Winter Proceedings of the Industrial Relations Research Association, 1967* (Madison: University of Wisconsin Press, 1968).

[3] Michael E. Borus, "Time Trends in the Benefits from Retraining in Connecticut," *Twentieth Annual Winter Proceedings of the Industrial Relations Research Association, 1967* (Madison: University of Wisconsin Press, 1968).

[4] Einar Hardin and Michael E. Borus, "Benefits and Costs of MDTA-ARA Retraining," *Industrial Relations* (May 1972).

[5] Earl D. Main, "A Nationwide Evaluation of MDTA Institutional Job Training," *Journal of Human Resources* (Spring 1968).

[6] Gerald Gurin, *A National Attitude Study of Trainees in MDTA Institutional Programs* (Ann Arbor: Survey Research Center, University of Michigan, August 1970).

rollees, but it did not use a control group or pursue economic variables. A pilot demonstration[7] of the application of the program planning and budgeting system to manpower programs drew for its information upon the reports emanating from the field to the national office. It used no control group, but estimated substantial improvements between pre- and posttraining annual earnings. The most careful study,[8] in terms of methodology, credited OJT with a significant increase in earnings for both men and women, while institutional training profited only men. However, despite its careful selection of a control group and commendable methodology, its sample was small, rural, geographically limited, and almost entirely black. Generalizing from it would appear to be hazardous.

Each of the studies, except Sewell's for institutional training, found benefits to exceed costs, but did so by assuming varying durabilities for earnings differentials observed for brief periods immediately following training. As pointed out in a study[9] by the Joint Economic Committee, hypothesizing only a five-year durability for the differential would have changed the results to negative for several of the studies.

MDTA institutional enrollees were also included in a sample drawn from a number of programs in Boston, Denver, and the San Francisco-Oakland Bay area.[10] Results were never calculated by program across the four cities, but may be summarized for MDTA in three of the cities. In that book, the sample size was 158 in Boston, 149 in Denver, 199 in San Francisco, with too few in Oakland to be useful.

In Boston, the sample was 21 percent black, 29 percent Spanish-surnamed, 50 percent other white, 37 percent male, 20 percent on welfare. The group averaged 9.8 years of education. They gained an estimated average $1,000 in annual earnings over their pretraining experience after an average eight-month enrollment in MDTA. Most of the

---

7 Allan H. Muir et al., *Cost Effectiveness Analysis of On-the-Job and Institutional Training Courses* (Washington, D.C.: Planning Research Corporation, 1967).

8 David O. Sewell, *Training the Poor* (Kingston, Ontario: Industrial Relations Center, Queen's University, 1971).

9 *The Effectiveness of Manpower Training Programs: A Review of Research on the Impact on the Poor*, Paper no. 3 of *Studies in Public Welfare*, a staff study prepared for the Subcommittee on Fiscal Policy, Joint Economic Committee, 92d Cong. (Washington, D.C.: U.S. Government Printing Office, Nov. 20, 1972).

10 Garth L. Mangum and R. Thayne Robson (eds.), *Metropolitan Impact of Manpower Programs: A Four-City Comparison* (Salt Lake City: Olympus Publishing Company, 1973).

gain was credited to higher postenrollment wages rather than to more stable employment. The Boston study provided an interesting contrast between the results of the MDTA training — averaging eight months' enrollment — and another institutional training effort under CEP, which averaged a little more than three months. The enrollees in the CEP program — 56 percent male, 59 percent black, and 25 percent Spanish-surnamed — began with pretraining earnings substantially below the MDTA group, and after gains of about $1,400 in average annual earnings, arrived at approximate equity with the earnings of the MDTA group. Whether that proves that the three-month training was done better, whether some aspect other than the training content was responsible for the gain, whether males make greater gains than females, or whether the types of jobs available to graduates of either program were similar and imposed a ceiling on earnings possibilities can only be conjectured.

The Denver MDTA group, with near equality in distribution between the sexes, the Spanish-surnamed, and other whites, with a few blacks and American Indians — all averaging a 10th-grade education — also experienced estimated annual earnings gains of $1,000. That gain in Denver was equaled among other programs only by the few Work Incentive (WIN) enrollees who entered the labor force after training. The Denver MDTA gains were more attributable to improved employment stability than to higher wages.

The San Francisco MDTA sample, averaging a 10th-grade education, was split roughly three ways between Spanish-surnamed, blacks, and Orientals; three-fourths were male. Recent Chinese immigrants graduating from language training programs contributed heavily to annual earnings gains of approximately $1,500. However, the four-city study had no control group, and its pre- and postenrollment comparisons need deflating by whatever would have happened in the absence of the program. Thus each of these evaluations produced generally favorable results but was marred by its small size, limited geographical scope, or lack of a really comparable control group. The Joint Economic Committee's study, synthesizing the other studies, agreed that the results had been positive, but advocated great caution in interpreting the results because of the deficiencies of the studies.

## OUTCOMES FOR 1969 ENROLLEES

A nationwide outcomes study,[11] chosen as part of the tenth-year package of evaluations, was conducted by Decision Making Information (DMI), a survey research firm with substantial attitude polling, opinion survey, and market research experience. Although this study is no less vulnerable than the others in its methodology, it is larger, more recent, and provides useful insights. The 5,169 persons interviewed during late 1970 and early 1971 were 83 percent of a systematic random sample of both institutional and OJT enrollees who left MDTA training, either by dropout or completion, during 1969. The sample was chosen from 40 nationwide sites. No control group was used in the study, partly because of cost and partly because of the difficulty of retrospectively identifying a group of nonenrollees with characteristics on the relevant variables comparable to the enrollees. Characteristics of the respondents and the households from which they came are summarized in Tables 2-1 and 2-2. Measurement of program outcomes consisted of a comparison between the pre- and posttraining situations of each member of the sample interviewed. Improvement in the employment stability and earnings of enrollees was the primary measure of success, though other criteria were noted.

As a substitute for a control group, wage and employment trends at each of the 40 sample sites (as well as nationally) were examined in an attempt to estimate what would probably have happened to the earnings and employment of the sample had they never enrolled in the program. Yet one can never be sure what the "no program" result would have been in the absence of a valid control group; nor is it easy to assure that a control group is really comparable upon all the relevant variables. Since no study of substantial size has ever produced an acceptable control group for any manpower program evaluation, it is only a matter of supposition that this can be done. Yet uncertainty will end only when such a study is made, accompanied by long-term, longitudinal follow-up.

## CHANGES IN ANNUAL EARNINGS

The average institutional enrollee in DMI's sample gained $1,826 in estimated annual earnings between the 16-month pre- and posttraining

---

[11] *MDTA Outcomes Study, Final Report* no. CAL-7778, prepared for the Office of Evaluation, Manpower Administration, U.S. Department of Labor (Santa Ana, Calif.: Decision Making Information, Nov. 1971).

## Table 2-1

### Personal Characteristics of Institutional and OJT Enrollees

| Category | Size of Subgroup | | Proportional Distribution of Subgroups | |
|---|---|---|---|---|
| | Institutional | OJT | Institutional | OJT |
| Total group | 3,467 | 1,702 | 100% | 100% |
| Sex: | | | | |
| Men | 1,655 | 970 | 48 | 57 |
| Women | 1,812 | 732 | 52 | 43 |
| Age: | | | | |
| Younger than 19 | 16[a] | 12[a] | 1 | 1 |
| 19 to 21 years of age | 450 | 277 | 13 | 16 |
| 22 to 34 years of age | 1,782 | 909 | 51 | 53 |
| 35 to 44 years of age | 572 | 255 | 17 | 15 |
| 45 and older | 647 | 249 | 18 | 15 |
| Education: | | | | |
| Less than eight years | 289 | 103 | 9 | 6 |
| Eight years | 323 | 141 | 9 | 8 |
| Nine to 11 years | 1,218 | 562 | 35 | 33 |
| Twelve years | 1,247 | 647 | 36 | 38 |
| More than 12 years | 390 | 249 | 11 | 15 |
| Race and ethnicity: | | | | |
| White | 2,101 | 1,075 | 61 | 63 |
| Black | 1,278 | 602 | 37 | 35 |
| Spanish-surnamed | 427 | 179 | 12 | 10 |
| Other | 88[a] | 25[a] | 2% | 2% |

[a] Exercise caution when interpreting results from these subgroups because of the small number of sample cases.

Source: *MDTA Outcomes Study, Final Report* no. CAL-7778, prepared for the Office of Evaluation, Manpower Administration, U.S. Department of Labor (Santa Ana, Calif.: Decision Making Information, Nov. 1971), p. 3.4.

periods (Table 2-3). The average OJT enrollee during these same time periods gained $1,614. Annual earnings gains for various subgroups are recorded in Tables 2-3 and 2-4.

The levels of posttraining estimated annual earnings were $3,473 and $3,849 for institutional and OJT enrollees, respectively. Estimated earnings are a composite of the proportion of total available time worked and the pay received per unit of time worked. Annual earnings were

## Table 2-2

## Household Environment of Institutional and OJT Enrollees

| Category | Size of Subgroup | | Proportional Distribution of Subgroups | |
|---|---|---|---|---|
| | Institutional | OJT | Institutional | OJT |
| Total group | 3,467 | 1,702 | 100% | 100% |
| Position in household: | | | | |
| Head of household | 1,940 | 910 | 46 | 54 |
| Other | 1,527 | 792 | 44 | 46 |
| Size of household: | | | | |
| One | 289 | 102 | 8 | 6 |
| Two | 590 | 282 | 17 | 16 |
| Three | 736 | 387 | 21 | 23 |
| Four | 642 | 355 | 19 | 21 |
| Five | 470 | 238 | 14 | 14 |
| Six or more | 740 | 338 | 21 | 20 |
| Language spoken in home:[a] | | | | |
| English | 3,394 | 1,684 | 98 | 99 |
| Spanish/Portuguese | 407 | 155 | 12 | 9 |
| Other | 160 | 98[b] | 5 | 6 |
| Welfare status: | | | | |
| Currently on welfare | 822 | 251 | 24 | 15 |
| Received welfare in past | 504 | 171 | 14 | 10 |
| Never received welfare | 2,141 | 1,280 | 62% | 75% |

[a] Adds to more than total group because of bilingual households.

[b] Exercise caution when interpreting results from these subgroups because of the small number of sample cases.

Source: *MDTA Outcomes Study, Final Report* no. CAL-7778, prepared for the Office of Evaluation, Manpower Administration, U.S. Department of Labor (Santa Ana., Calif.: Decision Making Information, Nov. 1971), p. 3.6.

estimated by multiplying the proportion of available time worked by 2,000 (roughly the number of hours available in a work year) by the average hourly wage rate. For example, if an individual had been out of the program for 12 months at the time of interview and had been employed during nine of those months (75 percent) and if the weighted average hourly wage rate of his job was $2.00, then

$$0.75 \times \$2.00 \times 2,000 = \$3,000$$

the estimated annual earnings after training.

Table 2-3

## Change in Estimated Annual Earnings for Institutional Enrollees
### (By personal characteristics)

| Category | Estimated Annual Earnings | | Change in Estimated Annual Earnings[c] |
| --- | --- | --- | --- |
| | Pretraining[a] | Posttraining[b] | |
| Total group median | $2,570 | $3,473 | $1,876 |
| Sex: | | | |
| Men | 3,119 | 4,039 | 1,886 |
| Women | 2,086 | 3,031 | 2,046 |
| Age: | | | |
| 19 to 21 years old | 1,807 | 2,941 | 1,990 |
| 22 to 34 years old | 2,623 | 3,502 | 1,716 |
| 35 to 44 years old | 2,723 | 3,904 | 1,924 |
| 45 years and older | 2,755 | 3,480 | 1,822 |
| Education: | | | |
| Less than eight years | 2,618 | 3,223 | 940 |
| Eight years | 2,367 | 2,545 | 1,010 |
| Nine to 11 years | 2,468 | 3,275 | 1,056 |
| Twelve years | 2,612 | 3,696 | 2,336 |
| More than twelve years | 2,822 | 4,075 | 2,326 |
| Race and ethnicity: | | | |
| White | 2,692 | 3,700 | 2,134 |
| Black | 2,388 | 3,123 | 1,436 |
| Spanish-surnamed | 2,400 | 3,714 | 2,542 |
| Other nonwhite[h] | $2,688 | $3,200 | $1,352 |

[a] Median for all those holding at least one pretraining job.

[b] Median for all those holding at least one posttraining job.

[c] Not equal to differences between pre- and posttraining estimated annual earnings medians because this represents earnings increase for all those employed after training whether or not they were employed before training.

[d] Exercise caution when interpreting results from these subgroups because of the smaller number of sample cases.

Source: *MDTA Outcomes Study, Final Report* no. CAL-7778, prepared for the Office of Evaluation, Manpower Administration, U.S. Department of Labor (Santa Ana, Calif.: Decision Making Information, Nov. 1971), p. 7.7.

The relative contributions of the employment stability and pay components are a significant factor in analyzing the sources of gain and those services which seem most important for specific enrollees. Fully one-third of the institutional enrollees but only 10 percent of the OJT

TABLE 2-4

## Change in Estimated Annual Earnings for OJT Enrollees
### (By personal characteristics)

| Category | Estimated Annual Earnings | | Change in Estimated Annual Earnings[c] |
|---|---|---|---|
| | Pretraining[a] | Posttraining[b] | |
| Total group median ............................ | $2,691 | $3,849 | $1,614 |
| Sex: | | | |
| Men .................................................. | 3,117 | 4,365 | 1,536 |
| Women .............................................. | 2,258 | 3,280 | 1,464 |
| Age: | | | |
| 19 to 21 years old ............................. | 1,923 | 3,328 | 1,952 |
| 22 to 34 years old ............................. | 2,765 | 3,995 | 1,656 |
| 35 to 44 years older ......................... | 2,918 | 3,866 | 1,282 |
| 45 years and older ........................... | 3,027 | 3,952 | 720 |
| Education: | | | |
| Less than eight years ....................... | 2,654 | 3,442 | 774 |
| Eight years ...................................... | 2,729 | 3,614 | 1,144 |
| Nine to 11 years .............................. | 2,660 | 3,671 | 1,324 |
| Twelve years .................................... | 2,714 | 3,983 | 1,662 |
| More than twelve years ................... | 2,674 | 4,235 | 2,366 |
| Race and ethnicity: | | | |
| White ............................................... | 2,772 | 3,994 | 1,678 |
| Black ................................................ | 2,564 | 3,581 | 1,438 |
| Spanish-surnamed ........................... | 2,325 | 3,687 | 2,032 |
| Other nonwhite[d] ............................ | $2,000 | $3,563 | $2,184 |

[a] Median for all those holding at least one pretraining job.

[b] Median for all those holding at least one posttraining job.

[c] Not equal to differences between pre- and posttraining estimated annual earnings medians because this represents earnings increase for all those employed after training whether or not they were employed before training.

[d] Exercise caution when interpreting results from these subgroups because of the smaller number of sample cases.

Source: *MDTA Outcomes Study, Final Report* no. CAL-7778, prepared for the Office of Evaluation, Manpower Administration, U.S. Department of Labor (Santa Ana, Calif.: Decision Making Information, Nov. 1971), p. 7.10.

trainees held no job in the training period, which averaged 16 months in length. Of the institutional "no job" group, 64 percent were women and 16 percent were under 22 years of age. Also, of the institutional "no job" group, 65 percent neither worked nor looked for work in the months before enrolling, one-fifth looked for work sporadically, and one of seven claimed to have searched continuously without finding a job. Thus 85 percent of the "no jobbers" (28 percent of all institutional trainees) can be reasonably assumed to have been out of the labor force most of the time prior to enrolling in institutional training. That fact facilitates analysis of the cause of earnings gains, but increases the difficulty of determining what would have happened to the participants had they not enrolled.

If all of those who held no jobs before training were assumed to be out of the labor force (a small overestimate), all of their gains in earnings could be attributed to increased labor force participation. The gains of the remainder are a composite of those emanating from steadier employment and those resulting from higher wages. Multiplying the average proportion of time worked in the pretraining period (times 2,000 hours) by the hourly wage gain supplies the higher wage components. The residual is the contribution of reduced unemployment. Table 2-5 factors the total annual earnings gain into these three components. Increased labor force participation was the primary source of earnings gain for both institutional and OJT, followed by higher hourly wages and improved employment stability, in that order.

### Differential Gains by Personal Characteristics and Program Services

As important as overall earnings contributions of MDTA participation, in many ways, is the answer to the question: Which services worked best for whom under what circumstances? A program unsuccessful overall might still be useful for some groups; failures might be attributable to attempting to serve the wrong groups with the wrong tools; and

### Table 2-5

#### Component Sources of Annual Earnings Gains

| Category | Institutional | OJT |
| --- | --- | --- |
| Total annual earnings gains | $1,876 | $1,614 |
| Increased labor force participation component | 1,035 | 693 |
| Higher hourly wages component | 572 | 462 |
| Improved employment stability component | $ 269 | $ 459 |

success might be amplified by more careful selection of target groups and techniques. While Tables 2-4 and 2-5 give us information on the earnings gains of institutional training and OJT, respectively, for enrollees with various personal characteristics, Tables 2-6 and 2-7 differentiate the gains by nature of the training programs.

As a general rule, those in the sample who had the highest pre- and posttraining earnings also made the greatest gains in earnings. This is contrary to the findings of some related studies which showed those with highest pretraining earnings to still be ahead after training, but for the gap to narrow through above-average gains by the low earnings group.[12] Therefore both earnings and gains were greater for men than women, the middle-aged rather than the younger or older, the better rather than the less educated, and white rather than black. Exceptions were those youth and women who held no jobs during the pretraining period and therefore made spectacular gains from a zero base. The only real surprise in the data was the gains made by Spanish-surnamed enrollees.

Sex and age contributions biased the results for household and welfare status. Those heads of households and nonrecipients for welfare who worked before enrollment made greater progress than their counterparts. However, for those not holding jobs in the pretraining period, the large gains of youth (not heads of households) and women (many of whom had been on welfare) brought the groups to near equality.

The relationship between length of training and economic gains experienced after training among institutional enrollees was strong. Change in annual earnings increased with longer training periods for all who secured a job after training. However, the relationship between length of training and earnings changes turned out to be much more muddled when only those who had jobs in both pre- and posttraining periods were considered. That is, institutional training programs of ten months or more were the most effective in bringing enrollees into the labor force, thus increasing their annual earnings. If we consider only those who worked in both pre- and posttraining periods, gains peaked at eight to nine months and four to five months of training.

For OJT enrollees (Table 2-7), the greatest gains came to those who had some employment experience before and after training and who also completed six to seven months of training. Change in annual

---

[12] Mangum and Robson (eds.), *Metropolitan Impact of Manpower Programs*, *op. cit.*

Table 2-6

Change in Estimated Annual Earnings for Institutional Enrollees
(By characteristics of training program)

| Category | Estimated Annual Earnings | | Change in Estimated Annual Earnings | |
|---|---|---|---|---|
| | Pretraining[a] | Posttraining[b] | Employed Both Pre- and Posttraining[c] | Average All Enrollees[d] |
| Total group median | $2,570 | $3,473 | $ 841 | $1,876 |
| Type of program: | | | | |
| Skills Center | 2,688 | 3,697 | 1,019 | 1,974 |
| Individual referral | 2,188 | 3,083 | 478 | 2,384 |
| Other group training | 2,546 | 3,426 | 806 | 1,804 |
| Occupation of training: | | | | |
| Health services | 2,558 | 3,843 | 1,108 | 2,994 |
| Food services/homemaking | 2,173 | 3,105 | 751 | 1,864 |
| Clerical/sales | 2,020 | 3,042 | 833 | 2,028 |
| Service trades | 2,500 | 2,575 | 424 | 1,188 |
| Mechanics/repair | 2,818 | 3,706 | 872 | 1,984 |
| Construction trades | 2,808 | 4,354 | 1,470 | 2,462 |
| Machine skills | 3,461 | 4,561 | 1,009 | 1,660 |
| Other skills | 3,265 | 3,659 | 445 | 418 |
| Nonskills | 2,121 | 2,452 | 164 | 870 |
| Completed training | 2,632 | 3,668 | 1,005 | 2,092 |
| Did not complete training | 2,358 | 2,588 | 402 | 772 |
| Length of training: | | | | |
| One to two months | 2,490 | 2,987 | 640 | 1,176 |
| Three months | 2,561 | 3,098 | 454 | 1,312 |
| Four to fiive months | 2,701 | 3,549 | 1,010 | 1,604 |
| Six to seven months | 2,463 | 3,440 | 927 | 1,692 |
| Eight to nine months | 2,552 | 3,764 | 1,206 | 2,496 |
| Ten months and longer | $2,713 | $4,041 | $ 826 | $3,214 |

[a] Median for all those holding at least one pretraining job.

[b] Median for all those holding at least one posttraining job.

[c] Not equal to differences between pre- and posttraining estimated annual earnings medians because this represents earnings increase for all those employed after training whether or not they were employed before training.

[d] Exercise caution when interpreting results from these subgroups because of the smaller number of sample cases.

Source: *MDTA Outcomes Study, Final Report* no. CAL-7778, prepared for the Office of Evaluation, Manpower Administration, U.S. Department of Labor (Santa Ana, Calif.: Decision Making Information, Nov. 1971), p. 7.19.

## Table 2-7

### Change in Estimated Annual Earnings for OJT Enrollees
### (By characteristics of training program)

| Category | Estimated Annual Earnings | | Change in Estimated Annual Earnings | |
|---|---|---|---|---|
| | | | Employed Both Pre- and | Average All |
| | Pretraining[a] | Posttraining[b] | Posttraining[c] | Enrollees[d] |
| Total group median ............... | $2,691 | $3,849 | $ 921 | $1,614 |
| Occupation of training: | | | | |
|   Health services .............. | 2,520 | 3,772 | 967 | 1,660 |
|   Food services/homemaking .. | 2,526 | 3,464 | 1,064 | 1,816 |
|   Clerical/sales ............... | 2,500 | 3,786 | 1,183 | 1,786 |
|   Service trades ............... | 2,333 | 3,426 | 899 | 1,508 |
|   Mechanics/repair ........... | 2,565 | 3,761 | 866 | 1,886 |
|   Construction trades .......... | 4,037 | 5,167 | 765 | 1,772 |
|   Machine skills .............. | 2,706 | 3,845 | 858 | 1,350 |
|   Other skills ................ | 2,500 | 3,824 | 1,126 | 2,102 |
| Completed training ............. | 2,715 | 3,933 | 991 | 1,658 |
| Did not complete training ......... | 2,586 | 3,364 | 475 | 936 |
| Length of training: | | | | |
|   One to two months ........... | 2,519 | 3,588 | 771 | 1,296 |
|   Three months ............... | 2,742 | 3,910 | 880 | 1,376 |
|   Four to five months .......... | 2,568 | 3,741 | 934 | 1,730 |
|   Six to seven months .......... | 3,021 | 4,410 | 1,297 | 1,648 |
|   Eight to nine months .......... | 2,583 | 3,750 | 751 | 1,828 |
|   Ten months and longer ....... | $3,289 | $4,125 | $ 876 | $1,126 |

[a] Median for all those holding at least one pretraining job.

[b] Median for all those holding at least one posttraining job.

[c] Not equal to differences between pre- and posttraining estimated annual earnings medians because this represents earnings increase for all those employed after training whether or not they were employed before training.

[d] Exercise caution when interpreting results from these subgroups because of the smaller number of sample cases.

Source: *MDTA Outcomes Study, Final Report* no. CAL-7778, prepared for the Office of Evaluation, Manpower Administration, U.S. Department of Labor (Santa Ana, Calif.: Decision Making Information, Nov. 1971), p. 7.20.

earnings, including those who worked during posttraining only, was greatest for programs of eight to nine months and four to five months.

Among institutional training occupations, health services paid off most handsomely, followed by machine trades, construction trades, food services/homemaking, clerical/sales and service trades, in that order (Table 2-6). However, this ranking was heavily affected by those entering the labor force through the training route, and thus favored occupations popular with females who were more likely to have been out of the labor force before training. Removing the effects of increased labor force participation brings construction trades to the top of the increase in annual earnings ranking, followed by health services and machine trades. Basic education and other training components unrelated to skills training were reasonably effective for activating those previously out of the labor force, but as would be expected, seemed to induce little change in wages or in employment stability.

Among OJT occupations, the miscellaneous skills category — which includes those trained in communications skills, data processing, office machine operation, and others — brought the greatest earnings gains, followed by mechanics/repair, food services/homemaking, clerical/sales, and construction trades, with service trades and machine skills listed at the bottom. This represents a different ranking from that of "successful" institutional training occupations.

In general, enrollees with a favorable attitude toward training realized larger and more positive changes in annual earnings following training than those whose attitudes were unfavorable. It was not surprising to find a high correlation between the values placed upon work and self-direction and the levels of aspirations of the individual and the size of the earnings gains. For reasons enumerated elsewhere, causations in this relationship may run both ways.

Of considerable interest is the relative effectiveness of class-size projects, Skills Centers, and individual referrals. Originally, MDTA projects were organized in class-size groups and were housed in public schools during off-hours or in rented facilities. Subsequently, Skills Centers were established to provide a range of training offerings accompanied by on-site orientation, counseling, placement, and other supportive services. More recently, individual enrollees have been referred to regular ongoing school courses, with tuition paid by MDTA. Nearly three of four institutional enrollees in the DMI sample received their training in class-size group training programs, one of four went to Skills Centers for training, while only 4 percent were identified as individual referrals. Of this small group of individual referrals, 81 percent were women; typically they were better educated than other enrollees and more likely to reside in small urban and rural areas. On the other hand, Skills Center participants were drawn largely from metropolitan areas, were more likely to be black, and were less educated than other enrollees.

Significant differences in earnings gains emerge when the participants are classed by the three program types discussed above (Table 2-8). The median income gain for individual referral enrollees was $2,384, compared with $1,974 for Skills Center enrollees, and $1,804 for those in class-size projects. Again, the largest proportion of these gains can be accredited to entry into the labor force and posttraining of those who had not held a job before the training experience. Apparently the individual referral was effective for bringing into the labor force a large number of better educated women who were previously outside it. Skills Centers were most effective for adding to the employment stability of those already in the labor force and for increasing wage rates.

The effect of program mix on posttraining experiences of institutional and OJT enrollees is also manifest in the completion rates and the enrollees' occupation of training. Institutional training completers experienced approximately three times the earnings gains of those who left the program before completion.

In OJT, the difference in earnings gains between completers and terminators was not as great, but still the former group gained almost twice that of the terminators. Termination for an OJT enrollee has a different meaning from that of a trainee in an institutional program because "termination" means that the OJT enrollee quit or lost his job. For institutional trainees, "termination" could mean that a training-

TABLE 2-8

Component Sources of Earnings Gains for Institutional Enrollees
(By type of training)

| Type of Training | Total Annual Earnings Gain | Increased Labor Force Participation Component | Higher Hourly Wage Component | Improved Employment Stability Component |
|---|---|---|---|---|
| Individual referral | $2,384 | $1,906 | $454 | $ 24 |
| Skills Center | $1,974 | $ 955 | $652 | $367 |
| Class-size projects | $1,804 | $ 998 | $562 | $244 |

related or other job was secured. However, the nature of the OJT training must be kept in mind. Ninety percent of the OJT enrollees, as contrasted with only 66 percent of those in the institutional programs, held at least one job in the pretraining period, and many were probably upgraded without changing employers. Approximately one of ten OJT enrollees interviewed about their training experiences was confused and said in effect: "I have never been enrolled in a training program!" The job, rather than the training content, was probably the focus of interest of OJT enrollees, and the length of training for the OJT enrollee was of uncertain relevance.

## MDTA and the Disadvantaged

Since 1966, the extent to which MDTA could be instrumental in improving the employment and earnings of those described as disadvantaged has been a key element in its evaluation. The DMI study offers some evidence, even though the data are unable to precisely identify the disadvantaged. Data on family income were not obtained, but the category of individual heads of household with pretraining annual earnings below the Social Security poverty minimum for families of their size is a reasonable surrogate. Age characteristics for those younger than 22 or older than 44, the less than high school education, and the minority group memberships were all identifiable, but the physical and mental handicapped criteria were not. Of the institutional sample, 69 percent met the disadvantaged criteria, as did 56 percent of the OJT sample, reflecting adherence to the 65 percent disadvantaged criterion, at least for the institutional program. Table 2-9 shows the results.

The disadvantaged started and ended behind the others in both proportion of available time employed and hourly wage rate, but made greater gains in both and in annual earnings. In fact, the relative gains of both the institutional and the OJT trainees who met the disadvantaged criteria more than doubled the gains of their nondisadvantaged counterparts. Nevertheless, the average disadvantaged enrollee was not raised out of poverty . . . the trend was simply from deep in the depths of poverty to near its upper ranges. While others might be disposed to celebrate a two-thirds increase in earnings, regardless of the level of the

Table 2-9

Relative Earnings Gains of Disadvantaged
and Nondisadvantaged Enrollees

|  | Institutional | | OJT | |
| --- | --- | --- | --- | --- |
|  | Disad-vantaged | Nondis-advantaged | Disad-vantaged | Nondis-advantaged |
| Pretraining annual earnings ........ | $2,036 | $4,032 | $2,212 | $4,209 |
| Posttraining annual earnings ........ | $3,363 | $4,732 | $3,862 | $5,078 |
| Earnings gain[a] .............................. | $1,210 | $ 596 | $1,413 | $ 628 |

[a] These earnings gains do not equal the differences between pre- and posttraining earnings because they are calculated for only those with at least one job in each of the two periods.

Source: *MDTA Outcomes Study, Final Report* no. CAL-7778, prepared for the Office of Evaluation, Manpower Administration, U.S. Department of Labor (Santa Ana, Calif.: Decision Making Information, Nov. 1971), p. 1.26.

base, the Joint Economic Committee found in this fact reason to doubt the usefulness of manpower training programs.[13]

*Other Measurements of Success*

While the primary objective was to increase the employment and earnings of the enrollees, a number of other success measurements are worth mentioning. The proportion of institutional trainees who received raises more than doubled from 10 to 22 percent between their pre- and posttraining jobs. Whereas 36 percent had received promotions in the pretraining period, 65 percent did so after training. Only 45 percent of those who had jobs were receiving fringe benefits before training, while 84 percent had jobs offering fringe benefits in the posttraining period. For OJT enrollees, the portion receiving raises rose from 11 to 29 percent, promotions rose from 34 to 76 percent, and fringe benefits rose from 43 to 84 percent. Gains, consistent for all age, sex, race, education, and occupation groups, were significant in relation to the hypothesis that disadvantaged persons tend to operate in a secondary labor market of low-pay, dead-end, high-turnover jobs and that manpower programs have been unable to help them break through to the primary labor market. To attack or support the hypothesis from the DMI study,

_____

[13] *The Effectiveness of Manpower Training Programs* in *Studies in Public Welfare, op. cit.*

we would find it necessary to break out the gains in promotions and fringe benefits by various trainee characteristics within the sample.

No notable improvement in the job turnover occurred, with the average job of the institutional enrollee lasting 9.4 months before training and 10.2 months after training. Both OJT and institutional enrollees were more likely to seek work when they were jobless after than before they had been trained, a development consistent with the hypothesis that many had used the program as a means of entry into the labor force. Yet men were more likely than women to seek work, blacks more likely than whites, the young more likely than the old. In addition, those with fewer years of formal education were more likely than the better educated to seek work when they were out of a job. The Spanish-surnamed were the most aggressive job seekers.

Of particular interest is the stability of employment in training-related jobs. Institutional trainees were more likely than those in OJT to have changed occupations between the pre- and posttraining periods. Tables 2-10 and 2-11 chronicle the proportion of enrollees by occupation working in their training occupation before and after training and at the time of interview. Four facts stand out: (1) the great variation in training-related placement and retention by occupation, (2) the fact that those occupations characterized by rising demand rather than high

TABLE 2-10

Stability of Training-Related Jobs for Institutional Enrollees
(Percentage of total)

| Category | Occupation in Area of Training | | |
| --- | --- | --- | --- |
| | Pretraining | Posttraining | Current |
| Health services | 27% | 76% | 55% |
| Food services/homemaking | 27 | 46 | 30 |
| Clerical/sales | 25 | 63 | 43 |
| Service trades | 13 | 50 | 27 |
| Mechanics/repairs | 8 | 31 | 21 |
| Construction trades | 17 | 40 | 28 |
| Machine trades | 24 | 52 | 28 |
| Other skills | 30% | 40% | 33% |

Source: *MDTA Outcomes Study, Final Report* no. CAL-7778, prepared for the Office of Evaluation, Manpower Administration, U.S. Department of Labor (Santa Ana, Calif.: Decision Making Information, Nov. 1971), p. 9.26.

## Table 2-11

### Stability of Training-Related Jobs for OJT Enrollees
### (Percentage of total)

| Category | Occupation in Area of Training | | |
| --- | --- | --- | --- |
| | Pretraining | Posttraining | Current |
| Health services | 48% | 78% | 51% |
| Food services/homemaking | 44 | 58 | 33 |
| Clerical/sales | 52 | 61 | 42 |
| Service trades | 34 | 42 | 19 |
| Mechanics/repairs | 36 | 50 | 28 |
| Construction trades | 43 | 57 | 38 |
| Machine trades | 41 | 54 | 25 |
| Other skills | 11% | 22% | 20% |

Source: *MDTA Outcomes Study, Final Report* no. CAL-7778, prepared for the Office of Evaluation, Manpower Administration, U.S. Department of Labor (Santa Ana, Calif.: Decision Making Information, Nov. 1971), p. 9.27.

turnover alone — health and clerical — had the most favorable rates of training-related placement and retention, (3) the consistency in rankings between placement and retention in training-related occupations, and (4) the generally low level of that retention rate.

### Challenges to the DMI Study

If taken at face value, the DMI final report is generally favorable to MDTA, offering support for its continuance. However, lack of a control group in that study makes it impossible to be sure which parts (if any) would have occurred in the absence of the MDTA program. In addition, the report had not been released before it was challenged by the results of an analysis which used Social Security data. DMI had sought to obtain a matched sample from the Social Security Administration's one-tenth of one percent continuous work history sample (CWHS) as a control group, but was unable to do more than obtain data on its own sample as a check against the interview responses.

Shortly after DMI's analysis was completed, however, another preliminary comparison with Social Security data became available which sharply contrasted with the DMI results. Both of these Social Security data comparisons must be examined and efforts must be made to abstract from the impact of current trends in order to assess what is currently known about MDTA outcomes.

*DMI-Social Security Comparisons*

Table 2-12 compares the pre- and posttraining covered earnings data recorded by the Social Security Administration (SSA) with the earnings reported by the respondents to DMI interviewers for 4,976 or (96 percent) of the DMI sample identifiable from SSA files. The DMI reported earnings were substantially higher during both pre- and posttraining for all categories, except men enrolled in OJT. The earnings gains shown by the SSA data were substantially less than shown by the DMI survey, but with the exception of male OJT, were still substantial. Since Social Security data offer the best check available on the accuracy and dependability of the DMI survey, it is necessary to explore the possible explanations for the differences.

Reasons for some of the differences can be approached only speculatively. For example, information sources for the two documents were vastly different. The DMI survey relied on a former trainee's ability to

TABLE 2-12

Average Annual Earnings for Institutional and OJT Enrollees
as Reported by Social Security and Survey Data

| Category | Social Security Pretraining | | | | | Survey Pre-train-ing[a] | Social Security Post-training 1970 | Survey Post-train-ing[b] |
| | 1963 | 1964 | 1965 | 1966 | 1967 | | | |
|---|---|---|---|---|---|---|---|---|
| Males: | | | | | | | | |
| Institutional .... | $1,179 | $1,328 | $1,552 | $2,032 | $2,252 | $2,738 | $3,275 | $4,024 |
| OJT ................ | 1,092 | 1,309 | 1,578 | 2,139 | 2,468 | 3,321 | 4,281 | 4,339 |
| Females: | | | | | | | | |
| Institutional .... | 406 | 492 | 586 | 795 | 978 | 1,796 | 2,188 | 2,980 |
| OJT ................ | $ 492 | $ 555 | $ 642 | $ 903 | $1,171 | $2,292 | $2,611 | $3,105 |

[a] The survey pretraining period varied for each enrollee, depending upon when each entered the program during 1968–69.

[b] The survey posttraining period varied for each enrollee, depending upon when each left the program during 1969.

Source: *MDTA Outcomes Study, Final Report* no. CAL-7778, prepared for the Office of Evaluation, Manpower Administration, U.S. Department of Labor (Santa Ana, Calif.: Decision Making Information, Nov. 1971), p. 7.40.

recall his employment record over a three-year period. Faulty memories or a systematic response bias could have produced misleading data, the direction or magnitude of which is impossible to estimate.

Social Security data, while not subject to faulty recall, are limited in coverage. Most government and nonprofit organization employees were not covered by Social Security. An enrollee who at *any* time had covered earnings would have been included in calculating average annual income levels, even if he had not worked in covered employment during the tabulation years. Any earnings from employment not covered by Social Security would be reported in the survey but not in the Social Security-based data. Again, the magnitude of possible understatement cannot be determined. The time periods, both for pre- and posttraining, are also not identical for the two sets of data.

Two methodological differences are amenable to quantitative manipulation. First, by including with the survey averages the previously excluded no-job enrollees, we can calculate a new average with the same type of base as Social Security's. Second, DMI interviewers asked respondents about their employment status month by month. Anyone reporting employment in a particular month was assumed employed at the reported wage rate throughout the full month. Some may have been employed only part of particular months and only these actual earnings would be reported to Social Security. The probable influence of using only whole months in the survey calculations is a general overstatement of the actual time employed for many enrollees.

Adjusting for both these effects yields the new earnings estimates shown in Table 2-13. The new estimates for the survey data reduce the differences to a range that might be more comfortably explained by speculations regarding completeness of Social Security coverage or survey responses. Adjusted earnings increases reflecting all three components (change in labor force participation, wages, and employment stability) show less change than originally reported. There remains a $200 to $300 difference between the two sets of data. It can only be assumed that the true earnings change lies somewhere between the two figures.

Institutional enrollees therefore had about $1,300 to $1,500 average increases, with male enrollees increasing earnings by $100 more than female enrollees. Female OJT enrollees had an approximate $900

TABLE 2-13

Survey Average Earnings Data Adjusted for
Methodological Differences

| | Annual Earnings | | |
|---|---|---|---|
| | Reported by DMI | Adjusted DMI | Social Security |
| Institutional: | | | |
| Male — Posttraining | $4,024 | $3,482 | $3,275 |
| Pretraining | 2,738 | 1,908 | 1,908 [b] |
| Change | 1,886 [a] | 1,574 | 1,367 |
| Female — Posttraining | 2,980 | 2,458 | 2,188 |
| Pretraining | 1,796 | 972 | 972 [b] |
| Change | 2,046 [a] | 1,486 | 1,216 |
| OJT: | | | |
| Male — Posttraining | 4,339 | 3,983 | 4,281 |
| Pretraining | 3,321 | 2,808 | 2,808 [b] |
| Change | 1,536 [a] | 1,175 | 1,473 |
| Female — Posttraining | 3,105 | 2,802 | 2,611 |
| Pretraining | 2,292 | 1,835 | 1,835 [b] |
| Change | $1,464 [a] | $ 967 | $ 776 |

[a] Based on median data and not calculated as the difference between pre- and posttraining earnings.

[b] Based on Decision Making Information (DMI) pretraining income levels.

change in earnings, while the data for the males are less clear. If one accepts the possibility of incomplete coverage for Social Security earnings, then the actual change for this group would be in excess of $1,473.

## Social Security Before and After Training Comparisons

Another validity check of the favorable DMI report was the results of an as yet unpublished evaluation constructed entirely from SSA data. All available names and Social Security numbers were selected for institutional and OJT enrollees who had either completed or terminated MDTA training in 1964, the second full year of the program. Social Security records were recovered on 82 percent of them, allowing comparison of covered employment and earnings for each calendar quarter during 1958–62 as the pretraining period and the 1965–69 posttraining five years. A large control group was then selected from the CWHS and matched by the only variables in the Social Security records: age, sex, race, earnings levels, and earnings patterns.

On the average, the MDTA enrollees experienced pre- and post-training earnings gains which were less than those of the control group. If the results are to be accepted at face value, the MDTA enrollees were worse off than they would have been had they never enrolled. Broken down into subgroups, these data show that men and whites, on the average, had been penalized for enrolling, whereas women and non-whites had gained. That report is consistent with known facts discussed in a subsequent chapter. The bulk of MDTA training has occurred in occupations characterized by high turnover. For women, these were in the expanding health and clerical occupational areas. Men were trained predominantly in occupations such as automotive repair, machine operation, welding, etc., where high turnover was not accompanied by general expansion in employment. Women were often likely to be entering occupations previously not opened to them. Nonwhite men might also be finding a new entry route to jobs not easily available previously, whereas white men were not being offered anything as new in terms of opportunity.

The critical question for evaluating MDTA's outcome is whether the Social Security comparison was any more valid than the noncontrolled DMI comparison of pre- and posttraining. That enrollees were made worse off rather than simply being unaffected raises doubts. A further challenge was the fact that completers among the SSA sample clearly gained substantially over noncompleters — those eligible for the program who entered but did not complete it. If enrollees who finished were better off than those who started but failed to finish, why did they suffer in comparison to those with no connection to MDTA? Since the points of comparison — age, sex, race, and level and pattern of pre-training earnings — were meager, it is likely that the really relevant variables were not being controlled. The MDTA group might be more disadvantaged on such bases as education, family background, residence, and so forth, even though it was equal on the measured criteria. The control group was not a control group. Despite having gained somewhat widespread attention within federal policy circles, the study neither proved nor disproved MDTA's effectiveness.

*Earnings Contribution of MDTA*

What then can safely be said about MDTA outcomes? The substantial improvement in the annual earnings of MDTA participants is reassuring, but it does not prove that MDTA is responsible for those earnings gains. The issue is: What improvements in earnings resulted that would not have occurred if the enrollees had not been in the program? During the training and posttraining periods, wages were trending upward between 6 and 7 percent per year; and while the average elapsed time of 20 months from the midpoint of the pretraining to that of the posttraining period was taking place, the general wage level of the economy drifted upward 11 percent.

The wage increase experience of the 1969 enrollees was repeated for fiscal year 1971 and 1972 enrollees. If we compare the pre- and posttraining experiences of all terminees for whom records were available in the two fiscal years, we find that institutional enrollees gained 15.5 percent and OJT enrollees gained 14.6 percent in average hourly wages during fiscal year 1971, while the average hourly earnings of all production workers in the economy were advancing 5.9 percent. Institutional hourly wage gains were 8.7 percent in fiscal year 1972, compared to 6.3 percent for OJT and 4.1 percent for the average hourly earnings of all production workers. Percentage gains were roughly the same for whites and nonwhites, disadvantaged and nondisadvantaged, and family heads of household and nonheads of household for institutional enrollees; but for OJT enrollees, those with the lowest pretraining wages tended to make the greatest percentage gains.[14]

It is impossible to judge whether wages for MDTA participants would have risen more or less than the average; but if we assume that it is the average, approximately half of the wage gains might have occurred without the program. Nevertheless, because labor force participation and reduced unemployment together were more important components of earnings gains than were wages, deflating wage gains by the national wage trends would have left earnings gains of $1,621 for institutional enrollees and gains of $1,336 for OJT trainees. Unemployment was increasing throughout the nation, and in the study areas, the increase continued during the training and posttraining periods. The probability

---

[14] Office of Financial and Management Information Systems, Manpower Administration, U.S. Department of Labor, June 12, 1972.

of finding a job and being steadily employed was declining for the MDTA participant, as it was for any individual without a preexisting claim to a steady job — but it was particularly true for any person who found himself or herself queued up near the end of a hiring line. The improved employment stability of program participants, despite these economic conditions, was impressive.

It is equally difficult to determine what would have happened to the labor force participation rates of those previously out of the labor force had they not enrolled in MDTA. Some may have remained out of the labor force if the program had not provided a route of entry. Others would have entered regardless, but might have experienced more unemployment or lower wages in the process. (In that sense, attributing all of the earnings gains of this group to their increased labor force participation is misleading.)

Age and sex are the most important factors in judging what the no program labor force participation rates might have been. Most youth who had no job experience before enrolling in training would have entered the labor force eventually, whether or not the MDTA route was open, though they might not have had equal success in posttraining employment stability and wage rates. Those youth already in the labor force could have been expected to experience improving employment stability over a period of time.

As Tables 2-14 and 2-15 illustrate, increased labor force participation and improved employment stability account for all but a fraction

TABLE 2-14

Component Sources of Annual Earnings Gains
(By age group for institutional enrollees)

| Age at Time of Interview | Total Annual Income Gain | Increased Labor Force Participation Component | Improved Employment Stability Component | Higher Hourly Wages Component |
|---|---|---|---|---|
| 19 to 21 years | $1,990 | $1,176 | $648 | $166 |
| 22 to 34 years | 1,716 | 815 | 482 | 419 |
| 35 to 44 years | 1,924 | 940 | 579 | 405 |
| 45 years and older | $1,822 | $1,295 | $290 | $237 |

Source: *MDTA Outcomes Study, Final Report* no. CAL-7778, prepared for the Office of Evaluation, Manpower Administration, U.S. Department of Labor (Santa Ana, Calif.: Decision Making Information, Nov. 1971), p. 1.21.

Table 2-15

Component Sources of Annual Earnings Gains
(By age group for OJT enrollees)

| Age at Time of Interview | Total Annual Income Gain | Increased Labor Force Participation Component | Improved Employment Stability Component | Higher Hourly Wages Component |
|---|---|---|---|---|
| 19 to 21 years ........ | $1,952 | $909 | $815 | $228 |
| 22 to 34 years ........ | 1,656 | 551 | 661 | 444 |
| 35 to 44 years ........ | 1,282 | 593 | 306 | 383 |
| 45 years and older | $ 720 | $121 | $ 19 | $580 |

Source: *MDTA Outcomes Study, Final Report* no. CAL-7778, prepared for the
Office of Evaluation, Manpower Administration, U.S. Department of Labor
(Santa Ana, Calif.: Decision Making Information, Nov. 1971), p. 1.16.

of the earnings gains of the 19- to 21-year age group in both institutional
and OJT. The labor force participation component is the overwhelming contributor to institutional earnings gains, whereas the two employment components are about equal for OJT. Indeed, 43 percent of the
youngest institutional group and 13 percent of the youngest enrollees in
OJT never held a job during the pretraining period. All would have
undoubtedly entered the job market through other routes if MDTA had
not been available. It is difficult to know how much unemployment they
would have experienced in the process and what wage rates they would
have been able to command. Most of the group without pretraining
work experience, who were older than 21, probably faced some significant obstacle to labor force participation. Nearly two-thirds of the
institutional "no job" group were women, and 84 percent of this group
were older than 21.

Since labor force participation rates for white women fall rather
than rise between ages 24 and 35, and during the secondary peak from
ages 45 to 54, do not attain the height of the primary peak during ages
20 to 24, it is almost certain that MDTA enrollment resulted in a participation rate higher than it would otherwise have been for this group.
Nonwhite females show very little variation in participation rates from
age 20 to 54. The true increment from MDTA enrollment for all women
defies estimation. It is reasonable to assume that labor force participation for those who would have entered the labor force even without the

program was accompanied by more stable employment and higher wages than would have occurred without the training.

The large contribution to annual earnings gains made by increased labor force participation supports a suspicion sometimes suggested about training programs. Improved job skills should contribute to reduced unemployment and higher wages, but there is no inherent reason why they should contribute to labor force participation per se. Steadier employment and higher wages are an employer's decision, whereas labor force participation is decided solely by the employee. It might be that the MDTA program provided a route of labor market entry to which training was a peripheral appendage. On the other hand, the training may have been required for access to jobs and pay sufficiently attractive to motivate labor force participation. The fact that gains were correlated with length of training and completers outdid noncompleters suggests that training did make an independent contribution.

Since there is no way to determine the proportion of the labor force participation gain attributable to MDTA, we can only furnish an arbitrary summation: All of the earnings gains from reduced unemployment during a period of generally rising joblessness can probably be attributed to the program. If we discount for national wage trends, we see that half of the wage gains can also be credited to it. It is not unreasonable to assume that all of the youth would have entered the labor force but would have continued to experience unemployment at rates equal to those in the labor force before training and wage improvements no better than national trends. Deflated for labor force participation and wage factors, as well as the noted upward biases in the DMI data, annual earnings attributable to enrollment in institutional training would equal $1,250, while gains for OJT enrollees would have been $1,092.

*A Tentative Benefit-Cost Comparison*

Let us assume reasonable accuracy for these estimates . . . were the relationships between the benefits and the costs such that the program was worthwhile? Such comparisons confront philosophical, as well as statistical thickets. The DMI study gathered no cost data relatable to the programs in which the respondents were enrolled. Only general data calculated by dividing total MDTA financial obligations by total enrollments, completions, and placements are available (Table 2-16). More importantly, costs are imposed on taxpayers, whereas earnings

Table 2-16

MDTA Obligations, Enrollments, and per Capita Costs
(Fiscal years 1963–70)

| | Total | Institutional | OJT |
|---|---|---|---|
| MDTA obligations | $2,007,547,000 | $1,628,813,000 [a] | $378,734,000 |
| MDTA enrollments | 1,451,400 | 978,400 | 473,000 |
| MDTA completions | 987,200 | 651,700 | 335,000 |
| MDTA placements | 773,400 | 484,300 | 289,100 |
| Estimated costs: | | | |
| Per enrollee | 1,383 | 1,665 | 801 |
| Per completer | 2,034 | 2,499 | 1,129 |
| Per placement | $ 2,596 | $ 3,363 | $ 1,310 |

[a] Includes part-time and other training.

Source: *MDTA Outcomes Study, Final Report* no. CAL-7778, prepared for the Office of Evaluation, Manpower Administration, U.S. Department of Labor (Santa Ana, Calif.: Decision Making Information, Nov. 1971), p. 7.47.

gains accrue to enrollees, with some possible multiplier impacts upon the total economy. The latter are uncertain but are made doubtful by the likelihood that the jobs obtained by enrollees would otherwise have been filled by others. That is, MDTA participation does not increase total employment and national income but only shifts its incidence.

On the other hand, if broadening opportunity is the goal, some benefit ought to be attributed, even to those unsuccessful in gaining financially from the opportunity. The best resolution is simply to accept enhancement of the earnings of the target groups as the objective and measurement of benefit. Any possible earnings foregone by the enrollees during training can be ignored. OJT enrollees were being paid, while the average weekly institutional stipend of $60 a week was above the pretraining and likely training period earnings. If that is the case, Table 2-17 provides benefit-cost comparisons under various assumptions about discount rates and the number of years over which the earnings gains noted in the posttraining period might be expected to endure.

Since the earnings gains were calculated as an average for all enrollees, rather than for completers or those placed, the relevant comparison is with cost per enrollee. All that can be said for sure is that earnings gains endured for the first year after training. If they did no more

TABLE 2-17

Alternative Present Values of Annual Earnings Gains

| Discount Rate | Duration of Earnings Increment | | | | | |
|---|---|---|---|---|---|---|
| | One Year | | Five Years | | Ten Years | |
| | Institutional | OJT | Institutional | OJT | Institutional | OJT |
| Five percent ...... | $1,190 | $1,040 | $5,412 | $4,728 | $9,652 | $8,432 |
| Eight percent .... | $1,158 | $1,011 | $4,991 | $4,360 | $8,388 | $7,327 |
| Ten percent ........ | $1,136 | $ 993 | $4,738 | $4,140 | $7,681 | $6,710 |

Source: *MDTA Outcomes Study, Final Report* no. CAL-7778, prepared for the Office of Evaluation, Manpower Administration, U.S. Department of Labor (Santa Ana, Calif.: Decision Making Information, Nov. 1971), p. 7.50.

than that, only OJT paid its own way. But if the earnings gains experienced by the enrollees during the first year endured for as much as two years, the average benefits achieved by them were greater than the public funds spent in their behalf.

## MDTA OUTCOMES

The result of this lengthy recital may not seem worth the effort. The fact is that after 10 years, there is still no *definitive* evidence one way or the other about MDTA outcomes. Critics argue that only through comparison with a control group identical on all relevant variables will it ever be possible to say for certain how results for a treatment group differ from what would have happened in the absence of a program. Yet it is entirely possible that an unchallengeable control group may be impossible to construct.

Most of those evaluations which have produced employment and earnings comparisons have shown substantial gains between the pre- and posttraining periods or for enrollees over various control groups. However, the before and after comparisons always leave open the question of whether some other factor than the program participation was operative. Some of the control groups were challengeable; other studies were too limited for generalization. On the other hand, those studies which did reach negative conclusions have been at least as challengeable and less numerous than those which have defended the MDTA program.

Since the preponderance of the evidence has been favorable, it seems reasonable to list in that direction while seeking more definite evidence. There is no substitute for a carefully controlled, statistically sound, longitudinal study, even though it may be expensive and difficult to design and administer. Until such a study is undertaken and completed, MDTA's contributions will face continuing challenge, but it may be necessary to live with that uncertainty. The weight of the evidence is sufficient that no reasonable doubt of its worthwhileness remains. The average MDTA enrollee, both institutional and OJT, has experienced a substantial improvement in employment and earnings as a result of participation in the program. Average earnings remain at poverty levels, posttraining employment remains sporadic, but the improvement over pretraining conditions is impressive. The program has apparently been a good investment.

# 3

# MDTA Training Institutions

When MDTA was introduced in 1962, vocational and adult education were both under attack. Vocational education, it was charged, was geared more to the labor market of the early 1900s than that of the 1960s, and adult education was primarily avocational in nature ("basket weaving for bored housewives" is how one DOL official described it). Administrators of the system were said to be lacking in imagination, reluctant to update their curricula and methods of instruction, and oblivious to the accelerating technology change that was occurring in the American economy.

It is not surprising therefore that in the maneuvering that preceded passage of the Act, DOL fought hard to have the Secretary of Labor declared sole administrator of MDTA, thus blocking HEW's Office of Education from turning the program over to the "dubious" ministrations of vocational educators. For its part, USOE exhibited a surprising indifference to MDTA, but intense lobbying by the National Education Association and the American Vocational Association saved for the secretary of HEW responsibility for the training aspects of the Act, including designation of the training agents.

Within DOL, the Office of Manpower, Automation and Training — established to administer the proposed MDTA before passage of the Act — fought and lost a battle to gain control of the federal ES, whose state ES affiliates were responsible for the identification of training occupations and recruitment, screening, and selection of enrollees.

This battle marked the beginning of the end of the Office of Manpower, Automation and Training and paved the way for the reorganization of all manpower bureaus within DOL under a single Manpower Administration. The most significant result of both the congressional battle and the internecine warfare within DOL, however, was that the administration of the MDTA institutional training program was turned over to what many considered to be the most conservative and lethargic of public institutions: vocational education and ES.

No one can be certain in which direction the program might have veered had the Secretary of Labor been designated sole administrator of MDTA. It is improbable that a new education system, in competition with traditional vocational education, would have emerged; most likely the program would have taken on the characteristics of a large experimental and demonstration project, similar to that of the early Job Corps. Instead, the program proceeded at its own pace, and because its administrators restrained themselves from extravagant promises, it managed to avoid the limelight and the spate of adverse publicity suffered by later manpower programs funded under EOA.

The result is that the institutional training program began slowly, suffering in its early days from the strain of two agencies with vastly different mandates and operating procedures and attempting to design and put into operation mutually acceptable systems under which the program would function. USOE criticized the occupations identified by ES agencies; it claimed that DOL was unduly influenced by the labor movement, especially the garment and building trades, which made certain that training was not given in occupations controlled by unions. Others, including many within DOL, complained that MDTA was training in semiskilled occupational areas rather than in "new" and "growing" occupations. DOL countered that vocational schools were using the program to enrich their supply of equipment and that the training offered MDTA enrollees was second class. MDTA trainees could not be trained during prime hours because regular students occupied the shops and classrooms during those periods; curricula were not designed for an *adult* clientele, nor were instructors accustomed to dealing with adults.

Gradually, however, the two agencies learned to cope with each other and with the cumbersome dual-agency systems which were put into operation to administer the program. Starting with traditional pedagogy, the institutional training program changed at a gradually accelerating pace and eventually incorporated some of the most advanced educational and training techniques into its curricula. Today, the program is drastically different from what it was 10 years ago when the Act was passed, and it can claim part of the credit for the change which has occurred in the regular vocational education system over the same period.

Three types of projects evolved from the institutional training program:

(1) The separately funded, single-occupation, class-size project

(2) The multi-occupational project or Skills Centers

(3) The individual referral program

In the early days of MDTA, virtually all trainees were enrolled in single-occupation, class-size projects. Today, approximately 40 percent of all MDTA trainees are enrolled in multi-occupational projects or Skills Centers and 10 percent in individual referrals. At first the institutional program consisted solely of vocational skills training. Later, basic education and prevocational training were added, and with the advent of multi-occupational projects, such techniques as the "cluster approach" to vocational training, "spinoffs," individualized instruction, and the open-entry/open-exit concept were introduced.

## SINGLE-OCCUPATION, CLASS-SIZE PROJECTS

The initial assignment of MDTA institutional training was to retrain individuals, whose skills had become obsolete, in new skills which were in demand in their local communities. The training could have been provided in one of two ways: (1) trainees could have been referred to classes in existing institutions or (2) separate classes for MDTA enrollees could have been established. The first method would have made available a wider range of occupational offerings to MDTA enrollees, lower training costs, and the integration of MDTA trainees with regular students. A separate class pattern had been set, however, through the retraining program of the Area Redevelopment Act which preceded MDTA. In addition, many existing vocational classes were filled, enrollment was limited to a September starting date, training methods were controlled by the more leisurely patterns of full-time students, and instructors were reluctant to include with their regular student bodies adults who were being paid to attend. As a result, the separate project method was adopted.

So long as the MDTA clientele were composed mainly of well-motivated, nondisadvantaged heads of households, the separate project method worked reasonably well. There were, however, several serious problems that impaired the overall quality of the program. First, the potential trainee was being denied a meaningful occupational choice . . . either he accepted the training course being established or he remained unemployed. Secondly, this approach caused underutilization of MDTA resources. Dropouts could not be replaced, thus causing slots to remain vacant from two to 24 weeks. Finally, only enrollees who were apt to succeed in a traditional "school setting" could be selected for the program. Unemployed applicants in need of remedial education, or those who had either dropped out or been pushed out of the regular school system, were not considered fit candidates for MDTA training.

When in the mid-1960s MDTA's target changed from serving non-disadvantaged, displaced workers to serving the disadvantaged, MDTA administrators were forced to find new methods of providing training to a less employable group of enrollees, most of whom had limited labor market experience and were hostile to traditional school settings. As early as 1964, experimentation had begun with the "multi-occupational" project. The first such experiment took place in Knoxville, Tennessee, under the Area Redevelopment Act. School districts in surrounding counties lacked the facilities and resources to train enrollees in several occupational areas. Arrangements were made whereby the Knoxville school district could provide the training for the several counties, in *all* proposed occupations, under one roof.

Immediately after the trainees were enrolled, it was discovered that they had certain deficiencies in reading and mathematics, as well as health and family problems, and held unfavorable attitudes toward working in occupations and surroundings foreign to their experience. Because there was no actual money to pay for remedial services under this Act, such services were arranged mostly through volunteer help from the Knoxville public schools. Trainees were released from occupational training courses for brief periods and were tutored individually as well as in groups to help overcome their deficiencies.

A second such experiment was conducted under MDTA by the O'Fallon Technical School in St. Louis, Missouri. Building on the concepts developed in these projects, Dr. Howard A. Mathews, Director of the Division of Manpower Development and Training in USOE, issued instructions in the autumn of 1963 outlining the procedures to follow in developing multi-occupational and training centers. Until that time, a training project involving more than one occupation plus basic education and other components would have required a complete set of multiple forms, course outlines, and budgets for each occupation and component. Under the new guidelines, numerous occupations could be listed for one project, with estimates of the number of enrollees for each occupation training and total costs for all. Then it was recommended that where possible, these multi-occupational programs be housed in a single training center which could be supported by a continuation of such projects, could provide the needed supportive services, and could concentrate on the needs of the MDTA recipients. None of these innovations appears startling in retrospect, but in the context of financial controls and bureaucratic procedures, they were major departures.

## Multi-occupational and Skills Centers

Once the multi-occupational concept was accepted and guidelines for funding such centers had been issued, it became only a matter of time before such concepts as open-entry/open-exit (a trainee may enter at any time during the project year and leave whenever he is "job ready"), the cluster approach (training in several related occupations), individualized instruction (a trainee may proceed at his own pace rather than "keep up with a class"), spinoffs (enrollees can complete training at various skill levels of an occupation), and other innovations were introduced. The concept of a one-stop training center, or Skills Center, eventually evolved.

Skills Centers differ from multi-occupational centers in that they must meet certain criteria established by HEW and DOL. In return for meeting these criteria, Skills Centers are afforded a more stable financial base, including annualized base funding for key staff, facilities, and equipment. Multi-occupational centers may meet one or more of these criteria, but they cannot be officially designated as a Skills Center until *all* criteria are met. Among the more important criteria (those that relate to the nature of a Skills Center) are the following:

(1) The centers must operate in a defined service area.

(2) They must maintain a level of operation of not less than 160 slots.

(3) Training must be offered during prime time hours.

(4) The centers must provide a variety of occupational offerings.

(5) In addition to occupational training, the centers must provide the following:

   (a) Basic education

   (b) Communication skills

   (c) Bilingual or second language instruction

   (d) Employment counseling

   (e) Personal counseling

   (f) Job development and placement

   (g) Follow-up of center graduates

(6) In addition, the centers must either provide or arrange for:

   (a) Prevocational experience or orientation

   (b) General education development (GED) training (high school equivalency)

   (c) Access to child care

   (d) Assistance with housing and transportation

   (e) Other supportive services

(7) Centers must have separate identifiable administrative entities.[1]

Today there are 70 Skills Centers throughout the nation, serving approximately 23,000 enrollees, or 17 percent of all institutional enrollment. The combined Skills Centers and multi-occupational centers account for more than 40 percent of all institutional enrollment.

The seventh criterion listed above is interesting in the light of early MDTA battles. At the time the Act was legislated, it was charged that

---

[1] *Evaluation of Manpower Development and Training: Skills Centers, Final Report* (Salt Lake City: Olympus Research Corporation, Feb. 15, 1971), pp. 1-3, 1-4.

regular vocational schools were not competent to provide the training envisioned by MDTA. When MDTA's target population switched from structurally displaced workers to the disadvantaged, this charge was raised again: Can the public schools which had already failed many among the target population be entrusted with the mission of training the disadvantaged? The requirement that Centers maintain "separate identifiable administrative entities" reveals that USOE was sensitive to criticism concerning this criterion. Although the public schools would be the sponsors of most Skills Centers, the Centers would be administratively divorced from the local school systems. A major reason for this criterion was to establish a training setting which would not remind enrollees of their previous failures in regular schools. Thus the nation's "traditional" educators eventually recognized the weaknesses in the existing system and set out to establish a "subsystem" geared to the needs of those they had previously failed.

Although there has been no research conducted or evaluation made to date of the multi-occupational centers, a comprehensive evaluation of the Skills Centers was carried out by Olympus Research Corporation (ORC) between June 1970 and February 1971.[2] Since Skills Centers and multi-occupational centers share similar purposes and characteristics, it can be assumed that the results of the Skills Center evaluation apply generally to the others as well.

*Characteristics of Four Skills Centers*

One characteristic of a Skills Center is its diversity, both in terms of the trainees enrolled and its geographical location. Descriptions of four Centers in Philadelphia, Abingdon (Virginia), New York City, and Los Angeles illustrate not only this diversity but also how far the MDTA program has come since all trainees were enrolled in class-size projects in regular vocational schools.

A Philadelphia Skills Center:

> A seemingly endless brick warehouse looms to the right of the Schuylkill River Parkway not far from the exit to Pennsylvania Station. Huge white block letters proclaim: "John F. Kennedy Center for Vocational Education." The mammoth (750,000 square feet) facility, once a U.S. Marine Corps warehouse, is now a control center for the Philadelphia School Sys-

---

[2] *Ibid.*

tem, an apprenticeship training center for the local building trades, and a Skills Center for the disadvantaged. The Center has a distinctly "old city" industrial flavor. The school "principals" sit in foremen's offices, shop doors permeate the lobby and enrollees look more like workers than students. The atmosphere suggests anything but a school. The urban renewed downtown and the black ghettos on the north, west, and south sides of the city surround the JFK Center; its enrollees are primarily black, their music "soul," and the predominate accent "northern stacatto." [3]

A Virginia Skills Center:

The lady behind the desk at the Empire Motel is singing "Raindrops Keep Falling on My Head" in rich Appalachian. Not one smokestack or factory mars the southern Virginia valley's rustic landscape. Cows graze on hillsides, here and there is an occasional barn, and everywhere there are rolling farmlands, tractors, men in overalls, and high, white, clapboard houses. Halfway between the motel and the Barter Theatre (which began in the thirties offering Shakespeare for produce and livestock) is the Washington County Vocational School, Abingdon, Virginia's Skills Center. The school on a hill overlooking the valley houses a newly formed community college, a high school vocational program, and a Skills Center. The building is old but is immaculately kept and the shops are well equipped. The atmosphere is school. The enrollees are white (with few exceptions), the songs they hum are "country," and their accents are "hillbilly." [4]

A New York City Skills Center:

The walk from the Delancy Street subway station on the Lower East Side to the New York Adult Vocational School on Rivington Street is a walk into the nation's immigrant past. The neighborhood's brownstone tenements are as overcrowded today as they were circa 1900, and on a hot summer day people still lean out of windows and lounge on front steps. Children use fire escapes as monkey bars, and clotheslines, strung from window sills to telephone poles on pulleys, air the neighborhood wash. While sidewalk vendors haggle, the smell of spicy foods mix with the overripe odor of garbage too infrequently collected, and a babble in several languages blends with the sometimes jarring traffic noises. When Senator Jacob Javits and Eddie Cantor were growing up in this area, the East Side was predominately Jewish. The synagogues are still there and orthodox rabbis are still in evi-

[3] *Ibid.*, p. 1-1.
[4] *Ibid.*

dence, but the star of David competes with royal blue and gold paintings of the Virgin Mary, and evangelical storefront churches are wedged in between saloons and shops. The people are predominately Puerto Rican now, although there is a liberal sprinkling of blacks and poor whites. While the Skills Center's enrollment reflects the neighborhood, there is a disproportionate number of black enrollees. The facility is an abandoned [and condemned] multi-story school. The street music is a blend of flamenco, rock, soul and just a touch of jazz. The accents are New Yorkese and Spanish.[5]

A Los Angeles Skills Center:

The Los Angeles smog seems to be more ethereal, though no less deadly, than the industrial wastes that pollute the air of Manhattan. There is no subway to the East Los Angeles Skills Center in Monterey Park, and the bus service is poor. Los Angeles is the city of freeways and automobiles. The Skills Center, one of five in Los Angeles, is almost hidden by a wall of parked cars in front of the office. The facility is a low, one-story industrial building, and its corridors are bustling with action. Over 90 percent of the enrollees are Mexican-American and English as a second language is a major problem. The overall success of the training activity depends to a great extent on the relative health of the aerospace industry. The background music is "mariachi" and the language of the enrollees who gather outside the snack bar pickup is a mixture of Spanish and English.[6]

ORC visited a total of 19 Skills Centers. Based on these visits, researchers documented the characteristics of Skills Center enrollees and their parents. Assessments were made of the programs and Center management systems, and all existing information regarding performance and cost was tabulated.

*Genealogical Characteristics of Enrollees*

Most Skills Center enrollees are children of migrants to cities from rural areas and the South or children of immigrants from Mexico and Puerto Rico to northern and western states. Fifteen of the 19 sample Centers are located in the North, accounting for 90 percent of the total enrollment of the sample. Yet 70 percent of the parents of the enrollees were born either in the South (56 percent) or outside the 50 states of

---

[5] *Ibid.*, pp. 1-1, 1-2.

[6] *Ibid.*, p. 1-2.

the United States (14 percent). Fifty-five percent of the parents were born in rural areas. Other parental characteristics are as follows:

(1) Thirty-six percent of the families of Skills Center enrollees were headed by either the mother or a nonparent relative, most often a grandparent.

(2) The average educational attainment rate of fathers was 8.9 years; the corresponding figure for mothers was 9.5 years.

(3) Nearly 60 percent of the families had four or more children; 20 percent had eight or more.

(4) The major occupational categories for parents were housewife, semiskilled worker, and laborer.

Skills Center enrollees were primarily of urban birth (66 percent) and were born outside the South, although a sizable percentage (41 percent) was born either in the South or outside the continental United States. The average educational attainment of Skills Center enrollees was 10.6, approximately 1.7 grades higher than their fathers and one grade higher than their mothers, but still substantially below the high school level.

An examination of other enrollee characteristics indicates the extent to which Skills Centers are serving the disadvantaged:

(1) More than 76 percent of all enrollees were listed as disadvantaged by ES.

(2) Nearly 70 percent fell below poverty income levels.

(3) More than 76 percent were members of minority groups.

(4) Nearly 60 percent were high school dropouts.

(5) More than 95 percent were listed as underemployed or unemployed.

(6) Forty percent were less than 21 years of age.

(7) Seven percent were 45 years of age or older.

(8) Fifty-three percent had been unemployed 10 weeks or more.

Skills Centers are serving a higher proportion of minorities than any manpower program except NAB-JOBS. They are serving more high school dropouts than other MDTA institutional and OJT projects and CEP, and more public assistance recipients than all programs except New Careers (and, of course, WIN). Considering that the MDTA institutional program can legitimately enroll 35 percent nondisadvantaged, while others are limited to the disadvantaged, Skills Centers compare favorably with other programs by this test.

*The Skills Center Program*

Though many instructional techniques adopted by Skills Centers and multi-occupational centers have been applied in some vocational schools, most have not been tested on a nationwide scale until now; nor have they been especially adapted to the teaching of the disadvantaged. In this sense, Skills Centers are laboratories for the teaching of employment skills to the disadvantaged. Instructional techniques are not static, theories are tested and discarded, and experimentation is encouraged. Program evaluation therefore is difficult. To evaluate a program constantly in transition is to fire at a moving target; it is never clear at what point an experimental effort can be fairly appraised. Nevertheless, after approximately six years of operation, Skills Centers and multi-occupational centers can be assessed.

*The Learning Environment*

Enrollees summed up the Skills Center teaching approach in a general consensus that trainees are treated more as adult working men and women than as students. For most enrollees, this approach does not present problems. The majority of Skills Center trainees seem well motivated and sincerely interested in acquiring marketable skills. In most Skills Center classes, however, there is a relatively large minority who are either hostile or indifferent. The mixing of these two groups presents a challenge to Skills Center instructors who have more flexibility than instructors in most other institutions; but they also face more pressure. While the ORC research team was on site, incidents occurred in six Centers which illustrate the kind of pressure Center staff and instructors face almost daily:

(1) One Skills Center director was unable to devote much time at ORC's initial interview because he was questioning four male enrollees who had been accused of raping a retarded female enrollee.

(2) In another Center, an instructor was physically beaten in front of his class by an enrollee who was enraged that the instructor had docked him a day's allowance for absenteeism.

(3) In still another Center, a male enrollee had his throat cut badly by the husband of a female trainee with whom he was keeping company. The husband and wife later in the day robbed two gas stations and fatally shot two gas station attendants.

(4) An enrollee went berserk during his lunch hour and was finally subdued by four policemen.

(5) The police appeared on site to arrest an enrollee for failure to pay more than 60 traffic violations; the enrollee could not speak English.

(6) A black director at one Center was attacked by a newspaper, printed by and circulated primarily among blacks, for firing a white instructor who led his black enrollees in a gambling operation in the classroom.

Although these events occurred while the interview team was on site at the various Centers, many other incidents were recounted to the team. For example, in one Center, which had a severe drug problem, an enrollee was shot at the Center by a pusher. The trainee (who survived) explained that he had refused to pay for what he considered "inferior stuff." Fast action by the director may have prevented a minor riot at another Center. Two white policemen parked in front of the Skills Center during lunch hour, when many trainees were milling around the front of the building, attempted to arrest a black enrollee. The enrollee resisted, and the policemen threw him to the ground. The Center director, who watched the incident from his office window, dashed outside and broke through the throng of enrollees who were circling around the two policemen. He physically pulled one of the policemen off the prostrate enrollee, lectured both policemen on their "stupidity," and promised personally to deliver the wanted enrollee to the police station. When the policemen agreed to this proposal, the director was able to convince the other enrollees to return to the building.

Incidents such as these are certain to have an effect on the enrollees' learning capabilities. One purpose of Job Corps is to remove a youth from a "bad" environment and place him in one which is conducive to learning. However, it soon became apparent in some Job Corps centers that many trainees were entering worse environments than those they had left. Similarly, Skills Center administrators have little or no control over their input. They must accept whoever is referred to the Center by ES, and ES is under pressure to fill slots with "the disadvantaged." Little screening or selection takes place. Inevitably, some "program hustlers" (enrollees interested mainly in allowances, not in training) and others for whom manpower programs are not the answer (drug addicts and alcoholics, for example) are enrolled.

Thus explosive situations are a way of life in most Centers. This factor, plus the inferior facilities and equipment (discussed subsequently in this chapter) and the narrow range of occupational offerings that are spelled out in the following paragraphs, has profound implications for the future of the Skills Center concept.

### Range of Occupational Offerings

Skills Centers and multi-occupational centers were designed to increase the range of occupational offerings to MDTA clientele. The evidence seems to indicate that although there is a wide range of occupational offerings in all 70 Skills Centers, the range in each Center is limited, and the same few courses account for the bulk of enrollment in all Skills Centers. The occupational range for women is especially limited.

Seven clusters account for 76 percent of total Skills Center enrollment: automotive mechanics, auto body repair, welding, production machine operator, office occupations, food services, and health occupations. Seventy percent of all female trainees are enrolled in only two clusters: office and health occupations. One reason for this deficiency may be the lack of labor market information at the local level. This subject will be discussed in detail in chapter 4. The requirement to train only in occupations where there is "reasonable expectation of employment," coupled with the need to keep per capita training costs low, encourages training in high-turnover occupations. An additional reason for this deficiency is the reluctance of Skills Center administrators to add or change course offerings. Additional courses would entail the purchase of new equipment, the storing of old equipment, the firing of instructors of discontinued courses, and the hiring of instructors for new courses. Skills Centers, like other institutions, tend to strive toward stability. They do not mind adding courses (providing that more funds are available), but understandably, they tend to resist deletion of existing occupational offerings.

*Course Quality*

All Skills Centers and most multi's are experimenting with the cluster approach, spinoffs, various methods of teaching basic education, and individualized instruction. All feature open-entry/open-exit courses and offer training in several occupational areas. A majority of Skills Centers offer prevocational training, language training, employability instruction, and GED preparation. The quality of training is by no means parallel throughout the Skills Center system; some Centers have highly developed instructional techniques, others must struggle. In most areas, however, Skills Center courses compare favorably to those offered in other vocational schools.

Skills Center instructional methods and techniques, on the other hand, are geared to the teaching of individuals who are far behind regular vocational and adult education students in educational achievement. They are institutions designed specifically to serve disadvantaged enrollees or enrollees who could not benefit from the traditional programs offered by regular public or private schools. Since no other such institutions exist — except perhaps for Opportunities Industrialization Centers (OIC) and the Operation SER program — comparisons between Skills Centers and most post-secondary adult education institutions are of limited validity. The two types of institutions have different overall purposes, clienteles, and methods for serving these clienteles.

The most successful courses in Skills Centers are in the following clusters: automotive (including diesel mechanics), welding, clerical, health, and production machine operator. Three clusters stand out as "problem" areas: food service, building maintenance, and sewing courses. These courses generally enroll the most disadvantaged. One ES official described them as the "dumping grounds" for the least employable applicants.

There are dangers in using any course as a dumping ground, but particularly such a course as food service. Many enrollees leave food service courses only to find themselves placed as low-paid kitchen workers or in similar positions, jobs which they could have attained before entering the Skills Center. Moreover, there is a great temptation to use food service for operations; i.e., for the preparation of meals for enrollees and staff. If this happens, as it often does, enrollees know they are in the "lower track." As a result, dropout rates climb and high-quality placements decline.

There are many opportunities for upward mobility in the food service industry, and Skills Centers could prepare people for those opportunities. One reason success seems to be limited in this field may be that both the quality of enrollee referred to food service courses and the quality of courses are too low to interest the better food service employers.

Building maintenance completers are also susceptible to placement in low-wage, menial jobs. The placement rate for building maintenance is the lowest for all occupational offerings (50 percent), and the course also has the highest absentee rate.

In spite of MDTA regulations excluding the garment trades, sewing courses are offered at many Centers (seven of the 19 visited by ORC), under various titles such as drapery worker or tailor. The same complaint is heard regarding these courses — placement in low-wage, menial jobs. Placement rates for these courses are also low, and absentee rates are high. Upholstery courses generally suffer the same experience.

*Basic Education*

The average school grade level attained by Skills Center enrollees in the 19 Centers included in the ORC sample was 10.4 years. The average achievement level was much lower. ORC was able to collect results from nine Centers which had recorded achievement tests. These Centers reported the average achievement level for both English and mathematics at the 6th grade level at the time of enrollment. One Center claimed to be able to increase reading and mathematics achievement one grade level in 14 to 18 hours of instruction. However, a nationwide study of basic education in MDTA, conducted by North American Rockwell Information Systems Company (NARISCO), revealed that it takes approximately 73 hours of instruction to raise the average enrollee one grade in reading and 82 hours for mathematics.

Basic education appeared to be most effective for enrollees who had achieved from 7th to 10th grade levels and received from 50 to 150 hours of instruction. It seemed relatively ineffective for those who tested below the 6th grade level.[7] The NARISCO study found that basic education instructors were inexperienced in the techniques they were

---

[7] North American Rockwell Information Systems Company, *MDTA Basic Education Program*, preliminary report, 1972.

attempting to use and handicapped from a lack of materials. They were confronted with a fundamental conflict in that individualized instruction was accepted as the best technique for basic education. However, motivation was greatest where the basic education was integrated with skills training; yet the two techniques seemed incompatible. These difficulties may have affected the results and made it difficult to draw conclusions that were universally applicable.

### Facilities and Equipment

The quality of facilities and equipment proved to be a major shortcoming and handicap to program effectiveness. Ten of the 19 Centers included in the ORC sample were located in industrial-commercial buildings. They ranged from new modern manufacturing facilities to surplus warehouses and one rundown hotel which was most recently used as a chicken hatchery. Five were in surplus elementary or secondary school buildings, four of which had been condemned. Two were in community colleges and two in area trade schools. Poor or inappropriate facilities proved to be not only damaging to the image of the program and the self-esteem of the enrollee, but were almost invariably *more expensive* than more attractive facilities. Rundown facilities are sometimes justified on the grounds that "grubby" physical plants are "what these enrollees are comfortable in" or "what prepares them for the realities of America's industrial work settings." It is doubtful that these justifications would be maintained if it were recognized that "no cost" savings results in the kind of situation described in the following report:

> Free or extremely low rent almost always translates into outmoded, inappropriate facilities that no one else wants *nor can afford*. It also means that staff costs will be higher because of the disproportionate number of employees required to maintain such facilities. It is simply not factual to say: "We must struggle along with these facilities because it's the best we can afford right now."
>
> The most inappropriate are usually those with the lowest rent and those which, but for the Skills Center program, would be abandoned warehouses, abandoned factories and abandoned public schools. Detroit's old factory and Philadelphia's old warehouse provide perhaps the best examples. Philadelphia's huge (750,000 square feet) ex-Marine Corps warehouse is an apparent bargain, with only 5 percent of the Skills Center's budget used for rent, utilities, etc.; but closer scrutiny reveals that approximately 25 percent of Philadelphia's total staff effort goes into maintaining and managing this vast facility. . . . On the

same basis, Detroit's apparent facility bargain (6 percent of total resources) actually consumes more than 25 percent of the Center's resources. In contrast, the Gardena (California), Des Moines and East Los Angeles Centers rent modern, competitively desirable, single-story, light industrial space in light industrial parks at competitive rental rates and still manage to spend about the average proportion of their budgets [13 percent] on facilities.[8]

Among the characteristics of Centers with high absentee rates is their location in traditional schools or converted military facilities; those with low absentee rates are generally located in campus-like or light industrial facilities. Other factors, such as the racial mix, the degree of disadvantaged enrolled, and the Center's policy regarding absenteeism, also affect attendance rates, but attendance rates are consistently higher in the better facilities and consistently lower in run-down facilities.

The primary reason that otherwise competent managers and educators rationalize the benefits of inappropriate facilities is that such facilities can be obtained at little expense and are used as local "in kind" matching . . . a clever gambit wherein all participants — government at all levels, the taxpayer, the program, and the enrollee — lose in the final analysis.

The primary factor influencing the quality of equipment available in Skills Centers is the inability of administrators to amortize the cost of equipment. All capital costs are charged against current budgets, a common practice in congressional funding of social programs in which is reflected the year-to-year "lease on life" that these programs must undergo. Initial capital outlays for most Skills Centers took place several years ago, with little or no replacement occurring since then. Program administrators, faced with decreasing funds, inflation, and pressure to increase enrollment, have reduced their capital budgets in order to maintain adequate staff to carry out programs. As a result, Centers have been forced into greater reliance on surplus equipment, whether or not it is appropriate. They have also shown resistance to any change in occupational offerings that might require heavy capital outlays. There also appears to be an unwillingness by administrators at higher levels to accept the fact that skills training, emphasizing shop experience, by its very nature requires heavier capital equipment budgets than most types

---

[8] *Skills Centers, Final Report, op. cit.*, pp. 5-31, 5-32. (Emphasis in the original.)

of education. The day of reckoning appears to be near. One can recondition and update obsolete and worn-out equipment for only so long before the quality of the program suffers. The average Center of the 19 in the ORC study spends only 4.7 percent of its total resources on equipment. Current facilities and equipment costs could be increased 50 percent or more with only marginal effects on total training costs.

## Counseling Services

No component of the Skills Center program is more difficult to analyze, classify, and prescribe for than counseling. There has always been worldwide debate in education on who should be called a "counselor" and the duties that should be ascribed to him. The uniqueness of the Skills Center program is such that the counseling experience, with its accepted definitions and rules of professional practice, may not be completely applicable elsewhere. Yet no component is more important to the success of the enrollee, the instructor, and the Skills Center itself — if it is skillfully applied.

Intercession is the essence of Skills Center counselors . . . for they often must intercede on behalf of the enrollees in such issues as the need for minor or major medical services, dental care, legal aid, child care, and so forth. Absentee rates would likely have skyrocketed had it not been for the presence and availability of Center counselors. Although it can be argued that such intercession cannot legitimately be called counseling, for Skills Center programs it is a necessary function; otherwise, many more enrollees throughout the years would have been terminated "for cause."

### Differences in Counseling

Counseling, as it is done in Skills Centers, differs markedly from that which is done in colleges, universities, or high schools because Center enrollees' needs are more basic and immediate. Counselors are almost constantly being pressured by instructors and administrators as well as enrollees. The following examples, quoted almost verbatim from a counselor who had been on the job slightly more than six months and one who had been a Skills Center counselor for five years, graphically illustrate the kinds of problems with which they are expected to grapple.

The Junior Counselor:

> On my first day, I reported for work at 8 o'clock in the morning. At 8:15, I was at my desk . . . [when] the phone rang.

It was the auto body instructor, and he said that he had a student who was high on heroin, and [asked if I would] mind talking to him. All kinds of thoughts ran through my mind, . . . what was I supposed to do with him, but all I said was "Send him down."

The guy came floating in and sat down. I introduced myself and he smiled. I don't know whether he was on heroin or not, but he was high on something. I ended up smiling back at him for about 10 minutes, and then I asked him to leave. He just smiled. What are you going to do in a case like that? Eventually, his brother came and took him home. He never came back. List him as a dropout. Well, ever since that first day, it's been more of the same.

The Senior Counselor:

Every Monday morning, a new crop of enrollees comes to the Center; and they bring problems with them that you wouldn't believe, like teeth that hurt so bad they can't concentrate, no place to sleep that night, and — no money, no money, no money! Some of them you have to take care of — if you can — even before you fill out the information sheet. Well, you've already got about 100 enrollees in here that are hurting, so what do you do? You try to take care of the ones that are hurting the most — and you don't succeed all the time, not by any means.

The problems of Skills Center counselors are aggravated by the simple fact that, considering the problems of the enrollees, there are not too many counselors. The ratio of enrollees to counselors in the 19 Centers was 73:1, ranging from a high of 181:1 to a low of 42:1. The ratio appears generous compared to high schools and post-secondary educational institutions where 400:1 is common. School counselors working under such ratios complain that they are able to find time only for those with serious multiple problems. But most Skill Center enrollees would be considered problem clients in a regular school system (indeed most of them *were* problem students when they were in the public school system). Counselors complain that enrollee-counselor ratios of this magnitude, when almost all enrollees are troubled, do not leave sufficient time to apply sophisticated counseling techniques.

In most cases the goals of Skills Center counseling operations have not been well articulated, nor does there seem to be much thought given to the purpose of counseling. Counselors generally create their own goals, based on whatever they may be doing at the moment. Most administrators do not understand counseling and are prone to assign "leftover" duties to counseling staffs. Counselors spend most of their time performing the following functions:

(1) Acquiring supportive services for enrollees (medical and dental care, child care, legal aid, etc.)

(2) Keeping attendance records and performing other disciplinary chores

(3) Counseling enrollees who are in trouble with instructors, or who have severe personal problems

### The Counselor as Disciplinarian

A major disciplinary chore performed by counselors is the keeping of attendance records, which in many instances means that an enrollee is "docked" a day's pay for an unauthorized absence or for excessive tardiness. Skills Center counselors disagree on the appropriateness of their roles as Center disciplinarians. Irrespective of how they feel, in most Skills Centers discipline is the counselor's responsibility. The intensity of the debate on the disciplinary role varies from picturing the counselor as a truant officer to seeing him as an advocate of the enrollee. Many cannot visualize him successfully playing both roles simultaneously. They argue that an enrollee is not likely to seek advice from a counselor who had previously cost the enrollee a day's pay for being absent.

Those who are against the assignment of any disciplinary functions to counselors maintain that as an enrollee advocate, the counselor cannot at the same time be a "law enforcement officer." Counselors in particular are opposed to the dual role. "Would you ask a policeman for advice about a personal problem?" one counselor asked an ORC researcher. The consensus among counselors in the 19 sample cities is that the disciplinarian should be "anybody but the counselor." But these counselors are quick to add that they are not arguing for a permissive approach to counseling. They believe strongly that a counselor can be more objective, even more stern, with enrollees if they are not saddled with the responsibility of discipline. "It's one thing to disagree with an enrollee," a counselor remarked, "it's something else to say, 'Do it my way or I'll punish you.'"

Surprisingly, many counselors disagree with the position stated above. They argue that counselors are the most appropriate disciplinarians because they *are* enrollee advocates. Instructors are more concerned with the success of their classes than with individual enrollees, and the chief concern of administrators is the overall record of the Center. If instructors and administrators have the final word about discipline, regardless of how strong an advocate a counselor might be, it is unlikely that the enrollee's position will be given sufficient consideration. One counselor said that instructors always think that they are given the "dregs of civilization"; he added that if they had their way, "half the Center would be terminated for cause." [9] Another said that instructors "like to justify excessive action on the grounds that this is a work situation. Well, it may be *like* a work situation, but it's still a school and these enrollees have hang-ups that deserve consideration." [10]

Interestingly, counselors both for and against disciplinary measures in their jobs argue the enrollee advocate point of view. Those against say that discipline-type chores vitiate their role as the enrollee's friend within management, while those for maintain that if discipline is turned over to instructors and administrators, there will be a lack of consideration for the problems and concerns of the enrollees.

It is difficult to take sides with either the pro or the con defenders, for they each express arguments that evince sagacity. From the point of view of administrators, instructors, and some counselors, the system is working well in most Centers. Yet most administrators and instructors do not understand the counseling function. Many believe that counselors would have nothing to do if they were not assigned specific responsibilities. For counselors who really want to "counsel," this attitude can be an irritant.

Those counselors who believe that discipline is an integral part of counseling and that it would be against the enrollee's best interest to relinquish the disciplinary function to either administrators or instructors have powerful arguments on their side. Having a built-in preference for orderly and quality training, administrators and instructors may tend to neglect the welfare of problem enrollees.

### Dual Counseling Responsibilities

Most Skills Center enrollees are served by ES counselors as well as those in Skills Centers. Theoretically, ES is supposed to supply "em-

---

[9] *Ibid.*, p. 4-12.
[10] *Ibid.*

ployment counseling," while the Centers should give "personal counseling." Because ES claims that its counselors are labor market experts, their efforts should be directed toward advising enrollees on labor market conditions, showing the best route for enrollees to take in obtaining and keeping a job in their particular trades, and other matters relating to employment. Personal counseling should be directed toward helping enrollees recognize and solve personal problems and adjust to the training situation. Although the theory is sound, the practicability is not, for it is impossible for a counselor to perform "employment" counseling without taking into account the personal problems of the enrollee. It is equally impossible for him to perform "personal" counseling without taking into account the realities of the labor market. As a result, both ES and Center counselors end up duplicating each other's efforts.

In addition, most ES counselors are *not* labor market experts: they are *counselors* and *expediters.* Nine Centers had ES counselors on site whose main function was to track down missing allowance checks or make corrections on enrollee forms which could have been causing mistakes in the amount of enrollee allowances. They also served as liaison officers between the Skills Center staff and the local office, and performed other paper work. They were counselors in name only.

There is general agreement at all Centers that most instructors know more about the labor market than either administrators or counselors, regardless of whether they work for ES or the Skills Center. The vast majority of Skills Center instructors have had years of experience in the skills they are teaching. They know what employers demand of their workers and what they are prepared to offer employees. They generally have excellent contacts within the various industries, and include, as part of their overall approach to teaching, tips on how to get and keep a job. Counselors, whether they be employed by ES or the Center, cannot match the expertise of experienced instructors.

The fact is that in most Centers where both Center and ES counselors work on site, the distinction between personal and employment counseling is ignored. Only one area ES office has insisted on the distinction and, to back up its position, has promulgated an agreement with the Skills Center administration to assign specific functions to ES and Center counselors. ES supervisors sought the agreement because they believed that ES counselors were being used as "rubber stamps" and that their expertise as labor market experts was being ignored. The ES counselors themselves, however, indicated that the agreement merely formalized existing procedures and that there is little real diffrence between their work and that of Center counselors.

In direct contrast to this situation, the East Los Angeles Skills Center entered into an agreement with ES which formally eliminated all distinctions between ES and Center counseling. All counselors at this Center, whether ES or Center employees, work under one supervisor and perform exactly the same functions. As a result of this action, counseling caseloads have been cut in half, and according to Center officials, the attempt by many enrollees to play one counselor against the other, a common occurrence under the old system, has been eliminated.

The latter action makes sense. It is a refreshing departure from bureaucratic "empire building" and is based on what is actually happening in the real world. It has resulted in benefits not only to the two agencies but, even more importantly, to the enrollees. The need for additional counselors is obvious. It makes little difference whether counselors are there because of Skills Center or ES funds since both come from the same MDTA source. The important thing is that there be an adequate number of counselors to serve the enrollees.

This agreement would not work, of course, if the two agencies involved insisted on supervising their particular employees. It is to the credit of both ES and the local schools in Los Angeles that such bureaucratic considerations have been put aside. The agreement stipulates that the counseling operation will be under the supervision of the Skills Center director. The supervisor of the counselors, however, is from ES.

*Supportive Services*

One of the guidelines for the designation of a Skills Center is that supportive services (such as medical aid, dental care, legal aid, child care, transportation, and similar services) be available to all enrollees. Since there is no budget for the provision of these services, they must be "promoted," or as the enrollees would say, "hustled." The designated "hustlers" of supportive services in all Skills Centers are the counselors. In two Centers, social workers help counselors fulfill this responsibility, and in one Center, three social worker aides are the lone counselor's sole support. In four Centers, school nurses help in providing minor medical care and promoting major medical care.

The acquisition of supportive services is both a source of satisfaction and frustration to counselors. Eyeglasses, free dental care, physical examinations, remedial medical treatment (both major and minor), psychiatric help, and help with drug and alcoholic problems have been provided to enrollees through the "hard hustling" of counselors, yet it is estimated that less than 50 percent of the need is met in the general medical field. Illness is one of the major causes of dropouts; not just illness of enrollees, but family illness as well. Counselors estimate that despite their best efforts, less than 30 percent of the need for child care is met, which probably accounts for "care of family" being another major reason for dropouts, especially among female enrollees.

Every Center has problems with alcoholism and drug abuse, some more than others; but even if only a small percentage of the total enrollment of a Center is involved, problem drinkers and possible addicts take up a disproportionate amount of a counselor's time. As one counselor put it:

> It takes time to discover whether or not a person is an alcoholic or drug addict. They just don't come out and tell you, and it's not as obvious as it might seem. If you do discover that you've got an alcoholic or addict on your hands, you just can't throw him out on the street. You have to try to find him help, or convince him to find help. And it's harder to find help for a drug addict or an alcoholic than for almost any other medical problem.[11]

One Center reported calling regularly on 20 agencies for supportive services, ranging from Alcoholics Anonymous through the school lunch program to planned parenthood. Some counselors have become experts in promoting free services from private doctors and dentists. Others concentrate on either providing legal aid or counseling enrollees on legal problems. Still others are unofficially designated as "community relations specialists," which means "hustlers of free services."

Vocational rehabilitation agencies provide help in some Centers; in others, counselors have discontinued referring enrollees for lack of response. In at least one Center, however, the state vocational rehabilitation agency has relieved counselors of the entire medical problem. All disadvantaged enrollees are enrolled as vocational rehabilitation clients. This means that their medical and dental needs are taken care of, not

---

[11] *Ibid.*, p. 4-11.

only while they are at the Center, but after they leave as well. In another Center, a vocational rehabilitation counselor spends part of his time at the Center. He has regularly scheduled meetings with enrollees in need of help and is able to direct some resources into the program.

The problem of providing supportive services to MDTA enrollees is one of the most difficult problems Skills Centers face. It takes up a greater portion of the counselor's time than any other activity, and despite heroic efforts by counselors, the need is not met. Other manpower programs are budgeted for supportive services, often using funds from MDTA budgets. Yet Skills Centers are denied the funds necessary to meet this obvious need.

*Administration*

Local on-site management of the typical Skills Center does not generally have the autonomy required by current guidelines, but has greater opportunity and freedom to innovate than traditional vocational education administrations. Erratic funding and budgeting procedures, together with restrictions on equipment, supplies, and facilities, are the greatest sources of day-to-day frustration for Skills Center management. In addition, the program can be seriously damaged by inferior recruitment, selection, assignment, job development, and job placement over which Center management has little or no control.

There is a wide variation in the quality and use of accepted management practices and devices throughout the Skills Center system. The better operated Centers generally use most of the traditional administrative instruments, within some framework of an overall approach, to successfully carry out their common mission. These Centers perform consistently better than those without well-defined, overall objectives and those which are overly controlled by off-site administrative structures.

Perhaps because on-site management has received little technical assistance, the Centers are particularly weak in generating, processing, and utilizing management information. This factor is aggravated by the absence of any adequate management information system. Fiscal and accounting practices are adequate for auditing purposes but cumbersome and devoid of useful management information, particularly true when the fiscal and accounting procedures are the primary responsibility of the sponsoring agency rather than on-site management.

In spite of all difficulties, and perhaps because of staff commitment to the Skills Center concept, local management of the Skills Center program is generally adequate and sometimes outstanding.

*Overall Conclusions*

Generally speaking, Skills Centers and multi-occupational centers are doing the job they were designed to do since they perform the following functions:

(1) In most areas, Skills Centers are the sole institutions both *capable* and *willing* to provide disadvantaged adults with skills training, supported by remedial education and supportive services.

(2) Skills Centers have proved their effectiveness in developing new methods and techniques for making institutional training more palatable for the disadvantaged.

(3) There is extensive evidence to indicate that Skills Centers have helped bring about change for the better in existing vocational education institutions.

(4) Skills Centers have helped develop a body of trained management and instructional staff who have expert knowledge in providing training to the disadvantaged and who are now in demand in more permanent institutions.

(5) Skills Centers have provided increasing opportunities for minority counselors and management personnel to develop their skills and find satisfying employment in the field of education.

(6) Skills Centers have demonstrated that it is possible to train individuals with entry-level skills in a considerably shorter period of time than it takes in most vocational institutions.

Although the six positive functions cited above are indicative of a well-ordered Skills Center, there are also negative factors to be considered. There are serious weaknesses in the Skills Center concept that must be recognized and eliminated if the program is to flourish in the future. Chief among these is that by concentrating on the disadvantaged, most Skills Centers appear to be "segregated" institutions. Inferior facilities and equipment and the narrow range of occupational offerings reinforce the image of a second-class education system for the disadvantaged.

Skills Centers and multi-occupational centers also suffer from an insecure financial base. As in all federally funded manpower programs, Skills Centers are subject to year-to-year appropriations and are affected by changing federal priorities in the funding of manpower programs. This year's "in" program ("in" programs in the past have included CEP, NAB-JOBS, and most recently, WIN) may affect allocations for the institutional program. The result is that organized planning and budgeting is impossible, funds available for capital outlay and facility acquisition are inadequate, and all staff operate in an atmosphere of insecurity.

It may be that the era of the separately established and administered Skills Center and multi-occupational center is coming to an end. The movement to integrate Skills Centers with nonsegregated community colleges has already begun in several areas, notably in Denver. The benefits to be derived from integrating Skills Center enrollees with regular community college students and the wider range of occupational offerings available to Skills Center enrollees such a merger makes possible have already been demonstrated. Unfortunately, in most areas, community colleges do not have the commitment to serve the disadvantaged. Nevertheless, Skills Centers may supply the needed leverage to pressure two-year, post-secondary schools into truly serving their communities.

Attention must also be given to providing a more secure financial base for Skills Centers. Since Skills Centers have already proved their worth in providing institutional training to the disadvantaged, there should be no further diversions of MDTA funds from Skills Centers and multi-occupational centers unless such diversions can be supported by documented evidence of cost-effectiveness or cost-benefit gains. This alone, however, will not solve the financial problems of Skills Centers. The program must begin to search for local or state tax support. The integration of Skills Centers with post-secondary educational institutions might help in this area, especially if MDTA funds can be used (as they were in Denver) to help support fledgling community colleges or to reorient existing state and local vocational educational institutions or systems.

## The Individual Referral Program

If there were doubts regarding the ability and willingness of existing post-secondary educational institutions to serve total communities —

including those who have suffered economic, social, and cultural deprivation — an assessment of MDTA's individual referral program would put them to rest. This program differs from other forms of institutional training in that it depends upon the willingness of existing educational institutions to accept applicants for MDTA training. If disadvantaged applicants are accepted, the program's success depends on whether or not school curricula are designed to meet the special needs of the disadvantaged.

A recent evaluation[12] of the program conducted by ORC reveals that individual referrals are growing not only in rural areas but in large metropolitan areas as well. The reason for the extensive use of individual referrals in rural areas is clear: The small populations with accompanying slot limitations make it difficult to launch class-size projects. However, the major reason for the increasing popularity of individual referrals in other areas is quite different: ES personnel believe that the individual referral method makes it easier to meet specific needs of individual applicants. Theoretically, by use of the individual referral method, existing private and public institutions can be used to provide a much wider variety of occupational offerings. The question remains, however, as to whether these institutions are designed to serve total community needs, including those of the disadvantaged. To the extent that this question can be answered in the affirmative, the need for Skills Centers and other special programs decreases. In fact, until this goal is met, the vast majority of disadvantaged will not be served at all; federal allocations for institutional training can meet only a small portion of the total universe of need.

ORC's evaluation, completed in June 1962 after nine months of study, concludes that the individual referral program is reserved for "preferred" enrollees. ORC researchers visited 92 individual referral institutions in 12 states, assessed the quality of training in those institutions, and assimilated all available performance and cost data.

*Enrollee Characteristics*

Table 3-1 compares the characteristics of MDTA institutional enrollees from national data, the individual referral study, and another

---

[12] *Evaluation of the MDTA Institutional Individual Referral Program, Final Report* (Salt Lake City: Olympus Research Corporation, June 1972), p. 33.

sample of all MDTA enrollees (except individual referral) in 14 cities. The following can be drawn from the table:

(1) The individual referral program shows fewer enrollees unemployed before training than do other MDTA programs.

(2) Enrollees in the individual referral program have more formal education than trainees in other forms of institutional training.

(3) The individual referral program is predominantly white.

(4) It is predominantly female.

To sum up, individual referral enrollees appear to be less disadvantaged than enrollees in other types of institutional training. Most individual referral institutions require that their enrollees meet the same entrance requirements as regular students, and most schools require a high school diploma.

*Program Characteristics*

As Skills Centers are geared toward providing training to the disadvantaged, so individual referral institutions are for the most part geared toward individuals who are most likely to succeed in a traditional school setting. The approach to education in most individual referral schools is traditional in nature, locked-step rather than individualized, lacking in innovative features, and bereft of remedial education, intensive counseling, and other supportive services. The facilities, equipment, material, and supplies of individual referral institutions, on the other hand, are far superior to those of Skills Centers and other class-size projects. Moreover, the range of occupational offerings in the individual referral program is far wider than that of any other institutional program. The individual referral program provides twice as many occupational offerings as the average Skills Center and eight times the number of courses offered in the average metropolitan area.

The *concentration* of individual referral enrollment, however, catering predominantly to women (62 percent), is in three occupational clusters: clerical and sales, health, and cosmetology. The concentration of enrollment in Skills Centers and other class-size projects, on the other hand, is in the blue-collar trades. The range of occupational offerings for women is relatively narrow (2,000 women enrolled in about a dozen occupational offerings) as compared to that of men (1,600 men in 177 occupational offerings).

*Administration*

Allocations for the individual referral program are growing at a rate twice as fast as for all MDTA training (institutional and OJT) and are increasing at a rate slightly faster than that of all institutional training.

Table 3-1

Enrollee Characteristics Summary Comparison for a Variety
of Sample Populations
(Fiscal 1971)

| | National Data | | | | 14 City Non-IR Sample |
|---|---|---|---|---|---|
| | Total Institutional Enrollees | Total Skills Center | Total Individual Referrals | 11 State IR Sample | |
| Sample size[a] | 131,989 | 22,839 | 11,851 | 1,350 | 1,304 |
| Disadvantaged | 66.3% | 74.6% | 67.6% | 67.4% | 68.7% |
| Poverty status | 63.4 | 71.5 | 68.4 | 75.1 | 67.6 |
| Family status: | | | | | |
|   Head of household | 58.1 | 56.6 | 63.6 | 62.4 | 58.8 |
|   Primary wage earner | 73.3 | 74.6 | 76.1 | 77.9 | 79.9 |
| Previous gainful employment: | | | | | |
|   3–9 years | 35.2 | 33.2 | 36.1 | 34.5 | 35.8 |
|   10 years or more | 18.7 | 16.3 | 17.1 | 16.4 | 15.6 |
| Employment status prior to enrollment: | | | | | |
|   Underemployed | 13.5 | 9.5 | 19.5 | 22.3 | 13.3 |
|   Unemployed | 72.7 | 85.9 | 73.1 | 72.5 | 74.4 |
|     15–26 weeks | 12.7 | 16.2 | 13.7 | NA | NA |
|     20–29 weeks | NA | NA | NA | 12.7 | 12.1 |
|     27 weeks or more | 23.8 | 27.0 | 24.0 | NA | NA |
|     30 weeks or more | NA | NA | NA | 28.0 | 36.3 |
| Hourly wage of last job: | | | | | |
|   Under $1.50/hr | NA | NA | NA | 20.0 | 11.6 |
|   $2.50/hr and over | NA | NA | NA | 25.6 | 29.4 |
| Education — years of school: | | | | | |
|   8 years or less | 12.4 | 12.4 | 5.8 | 4.1 | 9.2 |
|   9–11 years | 36.2 | 44.1 | 26.7 | 26.2 | 43.0 |
|   12 years or more | 51.4% | 43.5% | 67.5% | 69.7% | 47.8% |
|   (Average years) | (NA) | (NA) | (NA) | (11.5 yrs.) | (10.9 yrs.) |

## Table 3-1 (continued)

| | National Data | | | 11 State IR Sample | 14 City Non-IR Sample |
|---|---|---|---|---|---|
| | Total Institutional Enrollees | Total Skills Center | Total Individual Referrals | | |
| Race and ethnic data: | | | | | |
| White .......................... | 55.6% | 44.7% | 71.4% | 83.6% | 52.1% |
| Negro .......................... | 39.3 | 51.9 | 24.3 | 11.8 | 44.1 |
| Spanish surname .......... | 12.8 | 13.5 | 7.8 | 6.4 | 12.2 |
| Other minorities .......... | 5.1 | 3.4 | 4.3 | 4.6 | 3.9 |
| Age: | | | | | |
| Under 19 years ............ | 13.8 | 15.4 | 14.2 | NA | NA |
| 10–21 years ................. | 26.1 | 28.7 | 25.0 | NA | NA |
| 22–34 years ................. | 40.2 | 38.1 | 40.7 | NA | NA |
| 35–44 years ................. | 11.4 | 10.4 | 12.4 | NA | NA |
| 45 and older ................. | 8.5 | 7.4 | 7.7 | NA | NA |
| (Average) ..................... | (NA) | (NA) | (NA) | (27.8 yrs.) | (26.8 yrs.) |
| (Standard deviation) .. | (NA) | (NA) | (NA) | ( 9.62 yrs.) | ( 8.85 yrs.) |
| Public assistance: | | | | | |
| Total yes ...................... | 15.8 | 18.3 | 18.0 | 15.2 | 17.5 |
| Male yes ........................ | NA | NA | NA | 3.2 | 6.7 |
| Female yes ..................... | NA | NA | NA | 12.0 | 10.7 |
| Handicapped ................... | 11.1 | 11.1 | 14.9 | NA | NA |
| Veterans ........................ | 23.1 | 20.1 | 18.5 | NA | NA |
| Sex: | | | | | |
| Male .............................. | 58.5 | 60.0 | 46.9 | 45.3 | 58.8 |
| Female .......................... | 41.5% | 40.0% | 53.1% | 54.7 | 41.2 |
| Marital status: | | | | | |
| Married ......................... | NA | NA | NA | 33.7 | 32.6 |
| Not married ................... | NA | NA | NA | 66.3 | 67.4 |
| Number of dependents: | | | | | |
| No dependents ............ | NA | NA | NA | 45.4 | 51.6 |
| 1–2 dependents ............ | NA | NA | NA | 34.1 | 26.6 |
| 3–5 dependents ............ | NA | NA | NA | 16.7 | 18.2 |
| 6 or more dependents .. | NA | NA | NA | 3.8% | 3.6% |

NA = not available.

ᵃ This number = 100 percent.

Source: *Evaluation of the MDTA Institutional Individual Referral Program, Final Report* (Salt Lake City: Olympus Research Corporation, June 1972), pp. 56–57.

Once allocations for individual referrals have been approved at the regional level, administration and control of the program are the responsibility of the individual states. State administrations vary so widely that it is impossible to summarize the systems used. The results of monitoring and evaluation systems, however, if they exist at all, do not reach federal administrators. Individual referral allocations within states are generally based on geographical considerations. Most individual referral slots are distributed to rural or "balance of the state" CAMPS areas. The most effective use of individual referrals (in reaching applicants who otherwise would not be reached) is made in sparsely populated states.

*Private and Public Schools*

The individual referral program is the only MDTA component which makes wide use of private schools. Cost and performance comparisons between private and public individual referral institutions are contained in the next section of this chapter. Listed below are other major differences between the private and public schools included in the ORC sample (92 schools; 46 public and 46 private):

(1) The entrance requirements for private schools are stricter than those for public schools. Of the private schools surveyed, 50 percent reported that a high school diploma was required or preferred for acceptance into the institution. Only 26 percent of the public schools surveyed required enrollees to have a high school education. Fourteen public schools (in addition to six special individual referral programs administered by public schools) reported no entrance requirements.

(2) Only 35 percent of the private schools surveyed included basic education in their curricula (none of which could be considered remedial). Of the public schools, 83 percent include basic education in their curricula, the vast majority of which is nonremedial. Remedial education was featured only in programs created specifically for individual referrals.

(3) Sixteen public and 17 private schools (of a total of 92, equally divided between public and private) are open ended (that is, trainees can be enrolled at any time during the school year and terminated whenever they have become "job ready").

(4) The average length of training in private schools is 39 weeks; the corresponding figure for public schools in 56. The average hourly schedule for private schools is 6.1 hours per day; for public schools, 6.4.

(5) Of the 46 private schools surveyed, 34 do not employ counselors; 43 of the public schools do.

## Conclusions

Since the passage of MDTA in 1962, there have been major improvements in the nation's system of post-secondary vocational education. New systems of vocational-technical institutions and community colleges, as opposed to the more academically minded junior colleges, have been established in many states and some large metropolitan areas. Most of these schools have excellent facilities and equipment and relatively large budgets (in comparison to MDTA's modest appropriations for administration, instruction, and supplies). The experience of the individual referral program, which uses these facilities, indicates that they are not geared toward serving whole communities, including the disadvantaged. Skills Centers, multi-occupational centers, and other class-size programs remain the only alternatives in most areas for disadvantaged enrollees to acquire institutional occupational training.

The superior facilities and equipment of the individual referral program — together with its wider range of occupational offerings — reinforce the image of a dual educational system, a superior program for preferred enrollees, an inferior one for the disadvantaged. The issue as to why these tax-supported facilities are *not* available to *all* members of the community in need of institutional training is one which should receive policy-level consideration.

## COST-EFFECTIVENESS DATA

All available cost-effectiveness data regarding the institutional training program were compiled by ORC in its evaluations of the Skills Center program, the individual referral program, and the effectiveness of institutional training in meeting employers' needs in skills shortage occupations. Unfortunately, similar analyses have not been made of other manpower programs. This makes it impossible to compare results of the institutional program with those of other programs. Intra-program comparisons, however, are possible and the information is of some interest in and by itself.

Tables 3-2 and 3-3 give performance and cost information for the following:

(1) The mean for the total individual referral program in 12 sample states

(2) The mean for public individual referral schools

(3) The mean for private individual referral schools, excluding cosmetology

(4) The mean for 19 Skills Centers

(5) The mean for all institutional training (excluding individual referrals) in 14 metropolitan areas

Public individual referral costs are broken out from private school individual referral costs because public schools do not charge MDTA the full cost of training. Private school costs, on the other hand, do reflect the full cost of training. Cosmetology schools are excluded from the analysis because they also charge MDTA only a fraction of the true training costs; most cosmetology courses receive up to 80 percent of their operating costs from services provided customers by students.

It should be noted that cost information does not include allowances or nontraining Center-connected administrative costs. To arrive at an estimate of allowance costs, multiply the number of weeks of actual training indicated for each type of program by $60 (average MDTA allowance).

Tables 3-2 and 3-3 reveal that in terms of federal dollars expended for institutional training, the individual referral program is the least expensive in all categories. The overall cost of superiority of the individual referral program, however, is primarily due to the use of public schools which on the average charge the MDTA program less than the full cost of the training provided. The differences between private school individual referral costs and either Skills Centers or all institutional training are slight and can be accounted for by such factors as the amount of supportive services and counseling provided by class-size programs, the longer class hours, and the larger percentage of disadvantaged being served by Skills Centers and other class-size programs.

Table 3-2

MDTA Institutional Training Performance Data

| Category | Number of Different Occupations | Number Enrolled | Performance | | | Length of Training[a] | | Follow-up of Percentage Employed | | |
|---|---|---|---|---|---|---|---|---|---|---|
| | | | Per-centage Who Com-pleted | Per-centage of Com-pleters Placed | Placed in Train-ing-Related Jobs | Average no. of Planned Weeks | Average no. of Actual Weeks | 3 mo. | 6 mo. | Average |
| Mean for individual referral program | 189 | 3,033 | 65% | 48% | 79% | 40 | 30 | 69% | 71% | 70% |
| Public individual referral schools | 151 | 1,942 | 67 | 51 | 79 | 42 | 31 | 70 | 70 | 70 |
| Private individual referral schools — cosmetology | 87 | 1,164 | 63 | 36 | 77 | 35 | 25 | 67 | 74 | 71 |
| Average of 19 Skills Centers | 9 | 205 | 62 | 68 | 84 | (29–) | (20–) | 55 | 57 | 56 |
| All institutional MDTA in 14 cities | 6 | 192 | 61% | 56% | 81% | 25 | | 59% | 56% | 58% |

[a] All courses.

Table 3-3

MDTA Institutional Training Cost-Effectiveness Data

| Category | Average Training Costs per Enrolled Student | | Average per Man-Year Cost[a] | | Average Actual Cost | | | Average Cost per Employed[c] |
|---|---|---|---|---|---|---|---|---|
| | Planned | Actual | Planned | Actual | Completer | Placement[b] | | |
| Mean for individual referral program | $ 580 | $470 | $ 820 | $ 810 | $ 725 | $1,305 | | $1,042 |
| Public individual referral schools | 525 | 355 | 715 | 655 | 530 | 865 | | 755 |
| Private individual referral schools — cosmetology | 930 | 665 | 2,020 | 1,480 | 1,210 | 2,610 | | 1,705 |
| Average of 19 Skills Centers | | 850 | 2,880 | $3,250 | 1,400 | 2,210 | | 2,490 |
| All institutional MDTA in 14 cities | $1,030 | $930 | $2,380 | | $1,437 | $2,860 | | $2,420 |

[a] Projected to 52 weeks.

[b] Within 30 days.

[c] Based on the average of three- and six-month follow-up.

This leads to the interesting question as to whether MDTA is subsidizing the public schools or being subsidized by them. Should, could, or would public schools provide training for MDTA applicants without financial assistance from the federal government? Public schools can provide and are providing training to individual referrals at a lower cost (to MDTA) than the program could purchase from private schools. Nevertheless, public schools (which are supposedly free) are charging the federal government an average of $335 per man-year of training. Since many schools do not charge the MDTA program at all, it is obvious that some schools are charging well over the $335 average rate. Whether or not these costs are justified should be evaluated.

## SUMMARY

At the beginning of this chapter, we explained the process whereby MDTA institutional training was turned over to the administration of two of the nation's most conservative agencies — the public schools and the public ES. In 1962, it was only natural that the early advocates of MDTA would warn that the purposes of the Act would be frustrated by these "lethargic" agencies. Ten years later, the situation does not look so dark. A nationwide network of "new" educational institutions geared specifically to the needs of those whom the public schools had previously failed has been established, and ES has become far more client oriented than it has ever been in the past.

Thus MDTA's role in creating needed change in existing institutions cannot be underestimated. One other factor should be emphasized: Conservatives, by their very nature, are skeptical of panaceas and are not prone to making exaggerated promises. The MDTA institutional program, under conservative leadership, managed to avoid publicity. When multi-occupational projects and Skills Centers were introduced, there were no press releases. The program developed in comparative obscurity, thus avoiding the pressure that comes from close public scrutiny. On the other hand, the program developed slowly, *reacting* to new challenges, rather than *foreseeing* them.

It is possible, of course, that if progressives had seized control of MDTA in 1962, the program would have moved faster and would have put even more pressure on the public schools to improve their instructional techniques, facilities, and equipment. If we judge by the performance of other manpower efforts, funded under EOA, we see that the danger of progressive leadership might have been that expectations would have been raised too high, leading to failure as measured against impossible goals. Which would have accomplished the most is impossible to judge.

Much of the credit for the improvements which have been made in vocational education should go to MDTA. The individual referral evaluation points out that these improvements have not gone far enough: There has been a dramatic improvement in curricula (including expansion of occupational offerings), facilities, and equipment; but the programs are not geared toward *whole* communities. Entrance requirements are a major block to the disadvantaged, but even if they could gain admittance, the instructional techniques employed in most post-secondary schools are not designed for individuals who have suffered educational deprivation. So long as this condition remains, there will be a need for MDTA — especially Skills Centers and multi-occupational projects.

The MDTA individual referral program, although not geared specifically for the disadvantaged, could be a useful tool in providing training or retraining for veterans, displaced aerospace workers, and others who would fit into traditional school settings. The individual referral program is the closest to an educational voucher system in the manpower arsenal and should be used as such.

After ten years of experience, it can be said that the MDTA institutional training program has created a workable system for providing training to the disadvantaged, has helped create institutional change within both the public schools and ES, and has experimented with other means of delivering institutional training to all who need it. The ultimate goal, however, should be to eliminate the need for "special" programs. If this is to be accomplished, the public school system (especially community colleges and post-secondary schools) must make it possible for *all* members of the community to gain entrance to, and benefit from the educational services provided. Since most MDTA training is sponsored by the public schools, it should be possible to begin now to integrate MDTA training with that provided in permanent institutions.

# 4

# Impact of MDTA on the Labor Market

At the outset, MDTA had a twofold objective: first, its sought to use existing manpower resources efficiently; second, it visualized for occupationally displaced persons a retraining program whereby they could rejoin the mainstream of the employed with satisfying and remunerative careers. Although the MDTA program was initially based upon the assumption that there was too much "structural" unemployment that should be corrected, this assumption was never fully tested because shortly after the Act was made into law, unemployment rates began to decrease, and workers with labor market experience began to find jobs in occupational areas in which they were already trained, or they trained in new occupations.

As economic conditions became more favorable, it was soon apparent that those left without jobs were school dropouts, older workers, members of minority groups, and others who had never fully participated in the American economy . . . in short, the "disadvantaged." The result was that the second part of the major objective of MDTA was changed in 1966 from serving nondisadvantaged, displaced workers to serving the underemployed and unemployed disadvantaged.

In chapter 2, we appraised the extent to which MDTA participation had contributed to employment stability and earnings in the short run. Although the litany of evaluative materials cited in that chapter is profuse, there has been no sufficiently lengthy follow-up study with which to measure the longer term effects. In this chapter, we attempt to assess the extent to which MDTA has contributed to labor market efficiency. However, the conceptual and methodological obstacles loom even greater for this kind of evaluation than those which confronted us in the earlier chapter.

## Diffusion of Manpower Training Services

Before the MDTA program officially changed from serving non-disadvantaged workers to serving the hardcore unemployed and the so-called disadvantaged, experience was casting doubt on the efficacy of the original objective. Labor shortages did not seem to exist in occupations that were both attractive to enrollees and within the limited duration of MDTA training. If there were such jobs, there were no local labor market information systems capable of identifying them. When MDTA's concentration shifted to the disadvantaged, all pretense at retraining experienced individuals in new occupations was abandoned in favor of training the disadvantaged for *entry* into occupational areas where there was "reasonable expectation for employment" and which were "suitable" for institutional training. Unlike other manpower programs, however, the institutional program was allowed to retain 35 percent of its slots for training in "skills shortage" occupations.

By the mid-1960s, the MDTA program became one of a series of federally funded manpower programs designed to aid in the "war on poverty." All programs — Work Experience and Training, Neighborhood Youth Corps, New Careers, Job Corps, Operation Mainstream, CEP, WIN, etc. — were directed toward the disadvantaged. Some of the programs had specific target populations: CEP, geographical areas of high unemployment; WIN, welfare recipients; Neighborhood Youth Corps and Job Corps, youth; Operation Mainstream, indigent older workers. Some, such as CEP and WIN, incorporated all available manpower services under one overall sponsor; others concentrated solely on one manpower service.

In general, there are only four "payoff" components to all manpower programs: (1) institutional training, (2) OJT, (3) subsidized employment, and (4) placement services. All other components, such as counseling, job development, health care, legal aid, transportation, and other services, are supportive to the payoff components. To arrive at a proper "mix" of the four payoff components for any given area, we would have to know or establish the following:

(1) Criteria for selecting clients for each of the four components

(2) Characteristics of the target population, broken out by the selection criteria of (1) above

(3) Detailed occupational information at the local level and projected economic activity for local areas, including employment and unemployment rates

Some clients among the target population would be more suited to institutional training than OJT and vice versa. If unemployment rates are on the rise, allocations for subsidized employment or institutional training (which pays "allowances" to enrollees) should also rise, and allocations for OJT should decrease. Finally, if 35 percent of the enrollees in institutional training are to be trained in skills shortages, there should be some method available to local planners whereby they can *identify* "skills shortages."

These issues are not limited to the operation of MDTA; they relate to all manpower programs and manpower *planning* from the local to the national levels. Manpower planners depend primarily upon information emanating from state and local ES offices to justify the approach their programs take, and ES performs most recruitment and selection and referral for all manpower programs. Assessments of ES performance with regard to MDTA therefore would shed light on the quality of selection and referral practices and the quality of available labor market information throughout the entire manpower program complex. Three recent evaluations of MDTA cover these subjects in detail: ORC's evaluations of Skills Centers[1] and MDTA's skills shortage role,[2] and NARISCO's evaluation of MDTA systems.[3] All three evaluations point up serious deficiencies in the selection and referral process, in the availability of useful labor market information, and in the availability of

---

[1] *Evaluation of Manpower Development and Training: Skills Centers, Final Report* (Salt Lake City: Olympus Research Corporation, Feb. 15, 1971).

[2] *Evaluation of the Effectiveness of Institutional Manpower Training in Meeting Employers' Needs in Skills Shortage Occupations, Final Report* (Salt Lake City: Olympus Research Corporation, June 1972).

[3] *A Systems Analysis of the MDTA Institutional Training Program, Final Report* (Washington, D.C.: North American Rockwell Information Systems Company, March 1971).

performance and cost information for evaluative purposes. Though identified for the MDTA program, these deficiencies apply across the board to all manpower programs.

## Selection and Referral

What criteria are available to ES selection and referral officers or counselors with respect to which applicants should go into which manpower programs? The answer, according to the evaluations, is that none exist. It might be useful here to review the process an ES counselor goes through with an unemployed applicant.

The counselor has access to the following tools: (1) a Job Bank monitor in most areas, (2) ES job orders, (3) aptitude testing capability, (4) an application form filled out by the applicant, giving the applicant's work history, educational background, and other pertinent information, and (5) the counselor's own ability to establish a rapport that will help him gain an insight into the applicant's aspirations and problems.

The counselor's first order of business is to find the client a job. He scans the Job Bank monitor, looks through job orders, contacts job development personnel, and perhaps calls an employer or two he may know. If a job is not available, he checks to make certain that the applicant is eligible for whatever manpower or antipoverty programs may be available. Presumably, his interview with the applicant has given him some indication of the applicant's desires and qualifications or, more likely, lack of qualifications. Having ascertained that the applicant is eligible for an antipoverty program, he then checks to see which openings exist. He may then inform the applicant that there are openings at the Skills Center for, say, auto body repair and food service. The applicant may be indifferent until he is informed that an allowance is paid while he remains in training.

At this point selection and referral are implemented. The applicant who may never have entertained a desire to be an auto body man or cook may suddenly agree to "take anything." The counselor, who may have some doubts about the applicant's qualifications for either course, can: (1) schedule him for an aptitude test, (2) talk to him about future alternatives, or (3) enroll him in the Skills Center.

The counselor's actions depend upon several factors, not the least of which are his own talents, capabilities, and dedication, and the length of time that slots have been open. If the slots have been open for a long time, chances are that there is pressure on ES to fill them. And the counselor was most probably apprised of this fact by his supervisor that very morning. If he is a talented and dedicated counselor, he may ignore the pressure and do that which he thinks best, even if it means incurring the wrath of the applicant. If he is a normal human being, he may rationalize that training in a Skills Center is not going to *hurt* an applicant, so why not enroll him?

To determine how Skills Center enrollees enter the training system, interviewers asked ES selection and referral personnel in all 19 sample locations the following questions:

(1) What criteria do you use for referring applicants to Skills Centers?

(2) What tests are used to determine the fitness of potential enrollees for Skills Center training?

(3) What is the difference between these criteria and criteria for other manpower programs?

The answers revealed that no formal criteria exist for selecting applicants for various manpower programs, except for minimal education requirements needed for some institutional training courses. When possible, selection and referral personnel consider applicant preference, their own assessments of the applicants, or their own opinions of various programs. The major criterion for all manpower programs, however, is whether the applicant fits the definition of "disadvantaged."

The program to which the applicant is referred depends largely on the slots that are open at the time he applies. ES is constantly under pressure to fill slots. The selection process works best when a program is beginning and all slots are open. During this period, there is generally time for counselors to exercise some judgment in the referral of applicants to various programs. However, if ES is having problems in filling slots, the pressure mounts, and judgment becomes a luxury. Likewise, when slots open up while a program is in operation, ES is expected to act fast in filling those slots. Again, the search for "disadvantaged bodies" may be the only selection that takes place.

Thus, the criteria used by ES to select Skills Center enrollees do not differ appreciably from those used to select the clients of other manpower programs. CEP enrollees, of course, must come from a designated target area and WIN enrollees must be welfare recipients, but these "accidental" criteria have no bearing on the types of applicants that are most likely to succeed under various manpower strategies. ES counselors and selection personnel admit that inadequate assessments are made of enrollees before they are assigned to specific manpower programs. For example, aptitude tests are given to but a small number of applicants, and some local offices, reacting to bitter criticism of their testing policies by poverty groups, have discontinued aptitude testing altogether.

The services offered to the disadvantaged by various manpower programs overlap in some areas, but in most cases, are unique. Why then are applicant needs not matched, on a formal basis, with the unique services available from each program? There appear to be two reasons:

( 1 ) Very little research is done into the needs of client populations, or if it is done, generalizations about the kind of program best suited to subgroups within the target population are not made. Nor are criteria established which delineate the applicant needs each program is designed to serve.

( 2 ) The ever-present pressure is on ES personnel to fill whatever slots may be available at the moment.

All programs are expected to serve *all* disadvantaged applicants. The only significant instruction coming from the federal government to state and local administrators is that disadvantaged applicants should be referred to each program. No formal recognition is given to the fact that each of those that ES designates as Human Resource Development (HRD) applicants has specific needs, and that one program may serve those needs better than another. If the target population shifts to veterans or victims of economic downturns, the selection problem could become even more severe. Most manpower programs *are* designed for the disadvantaged, including most of the institutional training programs. It would take extensive revision to make existing programs suitable to the needs of nondisadvantaged workers with considerable labor market experience in responsible jobs, or for members of the military who have obtained experienec and skills in the service.

This brings into sharp focus an issue regarding manpower policy which deserves top level consideration. Too little attention has been given to *whom* programs are designed to serve and *what* they are supposed to do. It is not enough to state that the first priority is the disadvantaged. Programs must be designed to serve different needs within the disadvantaged population. Furthermore, even if the disadvantaged are given top priority, they must be served within the context of the larger population in need of services. For example, it may be that the disadvantaged cannot be adequately served unless there is a significant upgrading program in some areas. A fully articulated manpower policy would identify all — both disadvantaged and nondisadvantaged — who are in need of manpower services, and the kinds of services, broken down by subgroup, that are needed to adequately serve the entire population. After this has been accomplished, priorities, based on available resources, could be set and selection criteria issued to those responsible for selection and referral at the local level. Until this is accomplished, selection and referral will remain a weak and meaningless process.

## MDTA and Skills Shortage Programs

MDTA administrators are instructed to use 35 percent of available slots to alleviate skills shortages. In practice, it is obvious that the instruction is used only as relief from having to enroll a 100 percent disadvantaged population. Nevertheless, the skills shortage assignment is a useful starting point for appraising the labor market impact of MDTA. The first problem is a definitional and data problem. What is a skills shortage and how can it be measured? The literature of labor economics contains lengthy discussions of the terms "labor shortage" or "skills shortage," none of which ever achieved definitive results. In common parlance, a shortage exists when employers seek to hire more workers than appear ready to accept their offers. But why? Perhaps all workers with the requisite experience are already employed. But cannot demanding employers hire them away from their present jobs? Perhaps the apparent shortage is only unwillingness to offer the pay and nonpecuniary advantages necessary to attract workers from alternative activities. Few skills are in truth unique. If no one is available with the precise skills and experiences, can no one be attracted with adequate related skill? Skill requirements are noticeably flexible, rising in slack labor markets as people become available and loosening as jobs get harder to fill. Most production activities involve some combination of raw materials, capital, equipment, and human labor. What prevents the employer from compensating for manpower stringencies by changing these combinations? If not enough people with desired skills are available, why are employers not expanding training activities?

Perhaps time is the critical factor. Traditional static equilibrium analyses in which economists cross demand and supply curves abolish by definition the entire concept of shortages. At the equilibrium point, the number of persons employers are willing to hire at that wage is exactly equal to the number who are willing to work. The number "demanded" and "supplied" can diverge only when there is a gap between the wage offered and that expected, but the persistent tendency is to move toward equilibrium. However, in the real world, all adjustments take time, and there are disequilibrating as well as equilibrating forces.

The nearest labor economists have come to a satisfactory definition of labor shortage rests upon that time dimension. It is a situation in which the demand for labor in a particular occupation is rising faster than adjustments can occur, even though wages rise more rapidly than the average to attract workers from other pursuits.

The definitional problem for evaluating MDTA's skills shortage impact is twofold: (1) how the MDTA administrator, assigned to alleviate skills shortages, can identify them, and (2) how the evaluator can determine whether the administrator has been successful. As will be pointed out below, the problem of obtaining data on supply and demand is overwhelming; even if data were available, interpreting them would be even more difficult. The most that could be expected would be data on the number of employers seeking workers and workers seeking jobs in particular occupations. If the former exceeds the latter, is the problem lack of workers with requisite skills, relative unattractiveness of the job offers, institutional barriers which prevent matching supply and demand, or just the necessary time for adjustment?

Not only are data unavailable on job seekers and job vacancies, but employed workers might accept better jobs if they knew of them, and employers without explicit vacancies might hire extraordinarily qualified workers if they happened upon them. No central point exists at which those seeking either jobs or employees are identified and measured. The closest approach is the applications and job orders at the public ES.

Newspaper want ads, union hiring halls, and private employment agencies are other examples; but altogether they account for but a minor proportion of the total hiring transactions.

Yet even where employer job orders or worker applications are identified, no means exists for identifying "skills shortages." An accumulation of job orders in a particular occupation may mean:

(1) That the jobs, pay, and working conditions are not sufficiently attractive to lure workers

(2) That available or potential job seekers have not heard of the openings

(3) That the openings are in occupations which experience high turnover and a continuing need for new hires

(4) That the occupation is sufficiently large that openings are frequent, even though turnover is not high

(5) That barriers to the entry of available workers exist

(6) That there are, in fact, shortages of persons with the requisite skills to perform the required tasks

All of these issues are confronted in an attempt to assess MDTA's impact upon skills shortages. Many occupations wherein skills shortages might be expected require training beyond the reach of MDTA. Clerical and health occupations (areas of intense MDTA involvement) experience high turnover, even though they are relatively attractive jobs, simply because the incumbents are predominantly women. Low-skill, low-pay occupations in hospitals, restaurants, etc., are hard to fill because they are undesirable and are characterized by high turnover. Welding, the metal machine trades, auto mechanics, and auto body repair are not ordinarily high-turnover occupations but are so widespread that openings are usually available. Some complain that apprentice entrance requirements are too high and training too long, creating "false" shortages. Licensure, discrimination, or plain lack of information may block those who could perform the work.

Employers are constantly adapting to the available supply of labor — in the short run in their screening procedures, hiring requirements, and overtime practices; in the longer run, in redesigning jobs and designing and introducing technology. In that range of occupations within the scope of MDTA, shortages of experienced workers are much more likely than shortages of those with entry-level skills. And experience requirements are especially flexible, depending upon the relative status of supply and demand.

These definitions and practical problems set limits to the ability to answer the basic question of MDTA's impact on skills shortages. In any period, the possibilities would be only to identify occupations in demand and make judgments of the reasons for difficulty in filling those demands. By happenstance, ORC's study occurred during a recession and no employer interviewed reported having experienced a "skills shortage" in recent years. In fact, most admitted raising their hiring requirements as economic conditions declined.

Nevertheless, if MDTA is to have any effect on the labor markets in which it is operating, administrators must have some definition of what is meant by such terms as "skills shortage" and "demand" occupations and also must have some means for identifying them. Thus they must have access to comprehensive labor market information, including lists of job orders and occupational forecasts. In addition, for them to judge the "suitability" of various occupations for MDTA training, information regarding "preference variables," "hiring requirements," and the capacities of the client population must also be available. ORC's skills shortage evaluation therefore included an intensive review of the existing system for collecting, synthesizing, storing, and disseminating in a usable form labor market information for the use of MDTA planners.

## The Existing System

Underlying the operation of MDTA institutional training is a series of postulates:

(1) Training occurs in occupations where there is a demonstrable need or demand for trained workers.

(2) A body of knowledge necessary for determining these occupations exists.

(3) This knowledge resides within the ES system.

(4) It is extensive, accurate, stored, and retrievable in usable form.

(5) It is *used*.

The responsibility for determining which occupations to select for MDTA institutional training rests with ES. Its role as a broker produces a record of job market transactions more centralized than any other. Research staffs are trained to obtain, analyze, and interpret data pertaining to the workings of the labor market. Interviewing staffs are continuously involved in direct exchange with employers and job seekers, privy to special knowledge that accrues to people in direct, personal, daily contact. Finally, ES produces a massive quantity of written material emanating from its daily transactions. Thus, ES has the potential for establishing the most concentrated and sophisticated labor market system available in any community. The evidence seems to indicate, however, that this potential is far from being realized.

### Manpower Terminology

There is no commonly accepted definition of "skills shortage occupation" in the field. Skills shortage is used interchangeably with "demand" or "unfilled job order," and local office demand lists have little relationship to "demand" occupations. When asked: What does the term "skills shortage" mean to you? state and area research and statistics staffs exhibited utter confusion. Their answers varied from "lack of qualified applicants" to "impossible situation." Respondents in all 14 labor market areas included in the skills shortage study indicated that there is no official ES definition of skills shortage occupation, high turnover occupation, or demand occupation. A few elaborated on their answers by stating that there is no distinction made between high-turnover jobs, hard-to-fill orders, or shortage occupations.

In general, a rather simplistic view of shortage and surplus occupations dominates the field. By adding the demand factors (unfilled orders) in one column and the supply factors (applicants) in another column, and then subtracting the smaller figure from the larger, we arrive at a difference which constitutes "shortage" or "surplus." Though some efforts are made to identify the reasons for shortage (i.e., shortage of skills as against shortage of workers for other reasons), they are haphazard, inconsistent, and unscientific. There is no universally accepted tool or methodology for distinguishing between occupations in demand because of shortages of workers with requisite skills and those in demand because of high turnover and other factors.

### National Systems

Section 106(a) of the Manpower Development and Training Act directs the Secretary of Labor to develop "a comprehensive system of labor market information on a national, state, local, or other appropriate basis." The system is to include:

(1) The nature and extent of impediments to the maximum development of individual employment potential, including the number and characteristics of all persons requiring manpower services

(2) Job opportunities and skill requirements

(3) Labor supply in various skills

(4) Occupational outlook and employment trends in various occupations

(5) Economic and business development and location trends (to be done in cooperation and after consultation with the Secretary of Commerce)

In response to this directive, DOL has initiated several important programs, including:

The job order and labor turnover system (JOLTS)

The employment service area reporting system (ESARS)

The occupational employment statistics program

The occupational projections program

The employment, hours, and earnings (BLS "790" survey)

The unemployment insurance statistical reports

The ghetto job information program

The Job Bank printouts

The issue seems to be whether this information is complete for all users, whether it is put into a form which is understandable to users, whether it is distributed to users, and if so, whether it is actually used; and if not, why it is not. It is certain that most of the information emanating from national surveys is *not* useful to planners at the local level. However, the methodologies and sampling techniques used to perform these surveys almost certainly could be adapted for local use. There appear to be two reasons why this is not done: (1) ES research and statistics staffs are too busy doing the field work for national surveys, and (2) MDTA planning staffs have neither the time nor the expertise to install complicated systems for collecting labor market information at the local level. Underlying both of these reasons is an apparent assumption that the activities listed above are useful to local planners and are used. The vast majority of MDTA planners interviewed, however, stated that they had never heard of JOLTS, never examine Job Bank printouts (where Job Bank systems exist), never request services or information from ES research and statistics staffs, and use research and statistics publications only as "background verbiage" for proposals.

## Hard-to-Fill Order Lists

The nearest that research and statistics staffs come to producing "demand" or "shortage" lists are hard-to-fill order lists contained in *Area Manpower Reviews*. However, there is no uniform system for selecting occupations which appear on the lists. For example, in some areas, the lists are complete printouts of all unfilled orders for 30 days or more. No reasons are given for the orders being unfilled; no judgments are exercised. In other areas, the lists exclude low-skill, high-skill, and commissioned sales occupations. In some areas, the "list" is actually a narrative summary regarding certain occupational areas. In most areas, an attempt is made to explain why orders are unfilled, but the reasons given are generally too ambiguous to be of much use to planners. "Lack of qualified applicants" does not necessarily mean that "skill" is the quality lacking; it could easily relate to nonperformance factors, such as educational attainment, sex, or age. "Lack of qualified applicants with transportation" provides little insight into whether there is a skills shortage, but it may indicate a transportation problem.

The lists were quantified in only one of the labor markets visited; thus occupations with only one unfilled order had the same weight as occupations with 10 or more unfilled orders. With few exceptions, the lists represented only ES transactions.

These lists are unreliable for any purpose. In one city, "keypunch operator" was listed as a hard-to-fill job. However, an interview with the placement supervisor revealed that there were many highly experienced, skilled operators in the active file. When asked why "keypunch operator" was listed as hard to fill, the supervisor said that a fairly new employee had been given the responsibility for assembling the list, had been impressed by 10 openings, and had not checked the applicant file. The openings were poor, low-pay jobs.

In another city, Job Bank summaries were checked against the *Area*

*Manpower Review* list for the corresponding period. The Job Bank provided the following information:

| Occupation | Number of unfilled openings |
|---|---|
| Clothing salesman | 5 |
| Heavy truck driver | 3 |
| Lineman | 15 |
| Waitress | 1 |
| Cook | 1 |
| Presser | 1 |

Yet only the last three occupations were listed on the hard-to-fill list.

In still another city, the *Area Manpower Review* explained that hard-to-fill lists are based on transactions for the previous month. A total of 36 occupations, ranging in skill from nurse to service station attendant, were listed in the *Area Manpower Review*. Included also were two commission-type sales jobs, telephone solicitors, live-in maid, and porter. The Job Bank printout for the designated month listed no openings unfilled for 30 days or more, and its list of unfilled openings (for less than 30 days) was completely different from the list contained in the *Area Manpower Review*:

| Occupations on Area Manpower Review *list* | Number of unfilled openings |
|---|---|
| Guard | 2 |
| Porter | 1 |
| Main (live-in) | 2 |

| Occupations not on Area Manpower Review *list* | |
|---|---|
| Shirt presser | 4 |
| Cook | 4 |
| Billing clerk | 1 |
| Cashier | 1 |

It is possible, of course, that ES possesses a body of empirical knowledge about the quality of jobs and applicants, not reflected in transactions, which affects these judgments. Many ES interviewers intuitively feel that the published lists are of less value than their own judgments and knowledge. Admittedly, numbers alone are meaningless. However, neither quantity nor skill content of occupations appears to have consistently influenced decisions as to which occupations are placed on hard-to-fill order lists.

It seems a reasonable assumption that the research and statistics staffs of state employment security agencies and the labor market analysts in local ES offices could provide valuable staff services. Local operating staffs, including MDTA planners, would be the repository of relevant information about local labor markets. What other ES staff would have the focus, the trained personnel, and the facilities necessary to interpret and analyze a complex array of labor market information to determine shortages?

Appropriate research and statistics staffs were interviewed in all 14 areas. In four areas, the research and statistics function was attached to centralized state offices; only two research and statistics staffs were attached to local offices; and eight were attached to area or district offices.

The interviews revealed that research and statistics staffs were almost totally detached from the entire MDTA process. Apparently in the early days of MDTA, labor market analysts were required to "sign off" on all MDTA programs. As MDTA shifted toward training the disadvantaged and away from "filling shortages," these staffs were relieved of even that limited participation. Neither federal nor state guidelines require or assign any part of the process for identifying or justifying MDTA programs to research and statistics units. Thus such staffs in only four cities reported requests to perform special surveys for MDTA. Of the four, only one produces usable labor market information on a continuous basis for MDTA planners. The important point is that most operational staffs do not consider research and statistics a staff service designed to assist them and have no expectations that this component is available or equipped to serve their needs.

*Synthesis of Information*

Although occupational information comes into ES from many sources, including computerized data collection systems, this information is not analyzed, synthesized, and put into a form which would be useful to MDTA planners. Each order taken gives some information about an occupation. An accumulation of orders gives more. The flow of applicants, which is an important source of occupational information, includes a wide range of occupations — much wider than job orders, because of unemployment insurance registration requirements.

Employer relations interviewers learn something about the different ways skills are used by various employers and the kinds of skills the employers need. Occupational analysts, where they exist, provide in-depth information. Printed data, such as occupational guides, occupational projections, ESARS, JOLTS, etc., add to the flow of knowledge. Each of these represents a different focus, different kinds of information, different insights about occupations. Some would contribute knowledge about skills shortages or whether the apparent demand relates to other malfunctions in the market. Some would be helpful in determining the suitability of an occupation for MDTA training or, of even more importance, whether a segment of that market *could* be developed for MDTA training. The remarkable fact is that despite the introduction of computerized systems, there appears to be no design for storing, analyzing, and retrieving this kind of information. To improve local labor market information systems, priority should be given to the design of a system for drawing together existing information, emanating from many sources, in such a way that it would be useful to manpower planners.

*ES Transactions*

Most of the information used to justify MDTA training is based on ES job orders and placements. ES officials in 12 of the 14 cities responsible for writing requisitions or proposals for training programs (MT-1s) listed data from ES transactions as *the* major factor influencing their decisions. However, examination of ES listings in seven of the 14 study cities demonstrates that so long as ES transactions are the major justification for the establishment of institutional training programs, the range of occupations is bound to be narrow (Table 4-1).

Although there is considerable variance from city to city, this table clearly establishes that the concentration of ES job orders and placements is in a small number of low-skill, high-turnover jobs. For example, City A received a total of 7,887 job orders in 639 occupations during the survey month, but nearly 32 percent were in 14 low-skill, low-wage occupations. The same city made 2,832 placements in 395 occupations, but 36 percent were in 17 low-wage, low-skill jobs. If "tunnel vision" is to be avoided, some method must be devised for incorporating labor market information emanating from outside ES into local labor market information systems.

## The MDTA System

The ES is responsible for writing proposals (MT-1s) for MDTA institutional training projects. Theoretically, these proposals are supposed to be based on labor market or employer surveys and be reviewed by CAMPS or MDTA advisory committees, made up of employers and union and public representatives. Findings regarding this process are as follows:

(1) In only a few special cases were labor market surveys performed, and these only on a one-shot, noncontinuous basis.

(2) Employer surveys are sometimes performed (usually by telephone), but in most cases no record is kept of them; and those who make the surveys do not claim that they are statistically valid. Employer telephone surveys are generally conducted when a new project is being planned. Continuation of existing projects is generally based on performance records and a review of ES transactions in the occupational areas under consideration.

(3) CAMPS committees, in various stages of transition, have not been instrumental in supplying planners with potential occupations suitable for MDTA planning; nor have they received or asked for (in most cases) statistical justification for proposed training projects.

(4) MDTA advisory committees are either nonexistent or nonoperational in 12 or the 14 areas.

(5) Employer participation in planning has been mainly of a public relations nature. Employer interviews conducted by ORC (25 in each of the 14 areas) reveal that few employers make occupational projections or have substantial knowledge of the demand for workers in their own industries, let alone other industries.

## Table 4-1

### Distribution of Most Frequent Job Transactions
### (By occupation)

| City | Occupations of Most Frequent Openings | Occupations of Most Frequent Placements |
|---|---|---|
| A. | 31.9 percent of total openings in: Busboy/waiter, porter, light truck driver, kitchen helper, clerk-typist, secretary, service station attendant, warehouseman, cook, maid, arc welder, awning hanger, telephone solicitor | 36.0 percent of total placements in: Porter, busboy/waiter, light truck driver, kitchen helper, maid, warehouseman, service station attendant, cook, nurse's aide/orderly, clerk-typist, materials handler, electronic assembler, licensed practical nurse/-dental assistant, machine presser, hand packager, clerk (general), groundskeeper |
| B. | 46.6 percent of total openings in: Porter/casual laborer, phone book deliveryman, domestic worker | 54.8 percent of total placements in: Porter/casual laborer, phone book deliveryman |
| C. | 26.5 percent of total openings in: Domestic day worker, materials handler, maid, porter, yardman, busboy/waiter, maid (general) | 34.6 percent of total placements in: Domestic day worker, materials handler, yardman, maid |
| D. | 45.4 percent of total openings in: Materials handler, domestic day worker, warehouseman, kitchen helper, busboy/waiter, domestic maid, janitor/porter, watchman, clerk (general), sewing machine operator, lineman, bookkeeper, auto mechanic, switchboard operator, clerk-typist, general office clerk | 55.4 percent of total placements in: Warehouseman, materials handler, domestic day worker |
| E. | 52.7 percent of total openings in: Materials handler, sewing machine operator, porter, metal furniture assembler, hand packager, warehouseman, rubber plant laborer, heavy-duty truck driver, clerk-typist, busboy/waiter, instrument assembler, tin can laborer, clerk (general), office clerk | 25.8 percent of total placements in: Materials handler, metal furniture assembler |

Table 4-1 (continued)

| City | Occupations of Most Frequent Openings | Occupations of Most Frequent Placements |
|------|----------------------------------------|------------------------------------------|
| F. | 28.6 percent of total openings in:<br><br>Porter, busboy/waiter, nurse's aide/orderly, clerk-typist, high school teacher, secretary, mechanical engineer, kitchen helper, pipefitter/plumber, stock clerk, maid | 28.9 percent of total placements in:<br><br>Porter, stock clerk, clerk-typist, nurse's aide/orderly, busboy/waiter, janitor, brazing machine operator, warehouseman, secretary, materials handler |
| G. | 41.0 percent of total openings in:<br><br>Factory helper, construction laborer, kitchen helper, porter, materials handler, warehouseman, deliveryman, carpet layer's helper, busboy/waiter, maid (domestic), landscape laborer, carpenter, general office clerk, bricklayer | 43.1 percent of total placements in:<br><br>Materials handler, construction laborer, factory helper, kitchen helper, landscape laborer, warehouseman |

Source: *Evaluation of the Effectiveness of Institutional Manpower Training in Meeting Employers' Needs in Skills Shortage Occupations* (Salt Lake City: Olympus Research Corporation, June 1972), pp. 121, 122.

(6) Unions no longer participate actively in MDTA planning, but they are still considered a negative force by MDTA planners. Union-controlled segments of the labor market are considered "forbidden territory" by most MDTA planners, even those in "right to work" states.

*Guidelines*

One reason that manpower planning has fallen into disarray lies in in the fact that no national guidelines are currently in effect for the use of planners at state and local levels. Although the MDTA *Handbook*, written in 1962, outlines procedures to be followed in identifying occupations for MDTA training, it has been officially obsolete for several years. New national guidelines are being drafted but are not yet available. The *Handbook* sets forth detailed instructions for determining shortage occupations and selecting training programs, and it assigns a major responsibility to research and statistics divisions. However, the methods in the field have become totally different from those spelled out in the *Handbook*. In light of recent findings concerning operations in the labor market, the new methods are more pertinent to the problems at hand, but the lack of national guidelines allows these separate state and local entities to randomly choose their own methods for implementing MDTA programs.

Soon after the advent of MDTA in 1962 (with emphasis on training nondisadvantaged, displaced workers) labor market watchers realized that the program was not reaching the individuals it was meant to help. In 1964–65, changes occurred which compelled congressional committees to call for a more relaxed view of "reasonable expectations of employment." MDTA officials responded with a series of directives to the field, changing the emphasis as discussed earlier in this chapter. Research and statistics gradually was phased out. But the *Handbook* was not rescinded or replaced . . . it simply fell into disuse. No alternatives to the *Handbook* were developed; nor did the requirements on the MT-1 form change significantly. The report[4] on MDTA systems recommended the elimination of form MT-1.

The field received the message in a variety of ways, not the least of which was that the job of selecting occupations was given to minimally trained staff with limited experience in dealing with labor market information. The message clearly was that MDTA was now a vehicle for helping the disadvantaged get a job, not a vehicle for filling labor market needs. The two are not the same There is no way to use the placement of graduates as a measure to determine the extent to which MDTA is effectively providing workers with requisite skills in occupations where employers have needs. The field responded exactly as it was supposed to: The carefully designed methodology described in the *Handbook* was inappropriate, burdensome, and obsolete . . . except, no one actually said so.

The MT-1 form still requires that all questions be answered and all words be the "right" words. But those in the field are going through an exercise they regard as essentially futile and incongruous. MDTA staffs must shift for themselves. If information now being collected could be synthesized for the use of local planners, the situation would be much improved. If this were to happen, however, research and statistics staffs would have to be used. It would take the kind of sophistication and training possessed by research and statistics staffs to devise methods for

---

[4] *Systems Analysis of MDTA Institutional Training Program.*

synthesizing information coming from many sources — Job Bank printouts, JOLT, ESARS, unemployment insurance claimants, and so forth — in a manner which would be useful to planners at the local level. It would also take research and statistics expertise to devise methods for applying the national industrial matrix and occupational projection methodologies to local situations. Until this is accomplished, however, local ES offices will not become reliable sources of occupational information at the local or regional levels.

### MDTA Occupations and Labor Market Needs

In the previous section, we described the system (or lack of system) used for determining skills shortages and identifying occupations in which there are reasonable expectations for employment and which are suitable for MDTA institutional training. Three important factors which have a direct bearing on the material contained in this section emerged from this description:

(1) MDTA planners do not have available to them centralized sources of occupational information, nor do methods exist for distinguishing skills shortage occupations from those which may be in demand for numerous other reasons.

(2) Bits and pieces of occupational information *are* available to MDTA planners. These include: "hard-to-fill" order lists, computerized or hand-tabulated reports on all ES activities, occupational projections, area manpower surveys (in some areas), individual employer surveys regarding specific occupations, and suggestions from employers, unions, or committees.

(3) For the most part, MDTA planning is based on information derived solely from ES activities (although for new programs, employer surveys are conducted); information from the larger marketplace is generally lacking.

These points should be kept in mind while reviewing the material contained in this section.

### Major Findings

Searching for skills shortage occupations, ORC researchers examined hard-to-fill job orders and other data, performed want ad analyses, interviewed 25 or more employers in each of the 14 labor market areas, and interviewed local ES personnel, union representatives, state and local apprenticeship officials, and other involved and knowledgeable people about manpower conditions. The difficulties of defining and measuring skills shortages made it necessary to broaden the search to include those occupations in persistent demand which had substantial skill content.

In all, 905 occupations were identified which were in demand in one or more of the 14 areas. Those suitable for MDTA were segregated from the total, the extent to which MDTA training was already occurring in these occupations was measured, and the inhibitors preventing greater use of MDTA to meet the demands in these occupations were assessed. This analysis identified 156 occupations in demand, suitable for MDTA, not subject to overwhelming legal and political inhibitions and involving substantial skill content. But training had occurred in 88 of these, leaving an unexploited field of 68 occupations.

The analysis revealed the following:

Total demand occupations: 905

Unsuitable for MDTA by reason: 749, of which there were:

Outside legal scope of MDTA: 44

Lacking substantial skill content: 378

Trainable within allowable 104 weeks but not within current administratively limited length of training: 108

Union opposition: 77

Licensing and credentialing requirements: 5

Against MDTA regulations: 17

Employer hiring requirements: 7

Remaining occupations: 156, with

Number in which MDTA training occurred: 88

Suitable and uninhibited occupations without MDTA training: 68

Among the reasons for unsuitability, the first two do not inhibit the program but merely eliminate those occupations which require training beyond the 104 weeks authorized by the MDTA legislation or which do not involve sufficient skill content to justify institutional training. Licensing and credentialing regulations, national MDTA administrative decisions on appropriateness, and employer hiring practices are not major inhibitors of the institutional program. Only the brevity of training under current practices and union opposition loomed as significant inhibitors. Lack of a system for identifying demand occupations may be an inhibitor, depending on whether any unidentified shortages or demand occupations exist.

How serious are the shortages reflected by the 68 suitable but nontraining occupations? Why has not such training occurred? MDTA training rarely occurs for specific occupations. Thus the 68 nontraining occupations identified can be subsumed into seven clusters (Table 4-2), which in aggregate had been allocated only a little over 300 from a total of more than 11,000 MDTA slots available in the 14 areas within the three fiscal years studied.

Since funds spent for training in one occupation cannot be spent in another, the relevant question is: Why choose those occupations in which training occurred in preference for those which were suitable but

TABLE 4-2

Suitable Occupations in Which No Training Occurred
(Fourteen areas)

| Cluster | Number of Occupations | MDTA Slots |
|---|---|---|
| Draftsmen | 12 | 169 [a] |
| Nonmedical technicians and assistants | 17 | None |
| Bookkeeping and accounting | 5 | None [b] |
| Computer and data processing | 3 | None |
| Woodworking occupations | 18 | 80 |
| Truck and heavy equipment mechanics | 6 | 35 |
| Heating, cooling, and air conditioning | 7 | 30 |
| TOTAL | 68 | 314 |

[a] Most drafting is for one occupation: "mechanical draftsman."
[b] Excluding "accountant" or "CPA."
Source: *Evaluation of the Effectiveness of Institutional Manpower Training in Meeting Employers' Needs in Skills Shortage Occupations* (Salt Lake City: Olympus Research Corporation, June 1972), p. 11.

not chosen for training? Table 4-3 lists the occupations in which training occurred by their relative importance.

As the table indicates, 56 occupations accounted for more than 83 percent of all institutional slots in the 14 cities. In fact, 73 percent of the slots fell into five occupational clusters. Yet the narrowness does not indicate an absence of experiment or an unwillingness to broaden offerings. Training for occupations outside the basic areas is frequently attempted but rarely survives beyond one year. Completion and placement rates drop below existing norms, and administrators flee to the safety of familiar courses and predictable performances. Change is more likely where investment in facilities and equipment is less, but the fact remains that the persisting training occupations are those where completions and placements are more consistent.

Careful examination of the detailed occupations identified from the demand sources and those underlying the training clusters in the 14 areas suggests the following conclusions:

(1) MDTA was training heavily in five clusters which had high demand ratings: clerical, auto mechanics, welding, medical

TABLE 4-3

Overview of MDTA Institutional Training for Fourteen Areas
(Fiscal years 1969–71)

| Cluster | Number of Occupations | Number of Slots | Percentage of Total Slots |
|---|---|---|---|
| Clerical | 10 | 3,605 | 31.7% |
| Automotive | 13 | 1,360 | 12.0 |
| Medical occupations | 9 | 1,113 | 9.8 |
| Welding | 4 | 1,093 | 9.6 |
| Machine trades (metal) | 5 | 1,054 | 9.3 |
| Upholsterer/alteration tailor | 2 | 458 | 4.0 |
| Nonauto repair | 11 | 407 | 3.6 |
| Food services | 4 | 412 | 3.6 |
| All other | 32 | 1,865 | 16.4 |
| TOTAL | 90 | 11,367 | 100.0% |

Source: *Evaluation of the Effectiveness of Institutional Manpower Training in Meeting Employers' Needs in Skills Shortage Occupations* (Salt Lake City, Olympus Research Corporation, June 1972), p. 12.

occupations (except LPN), and mechanical drafting. It should be mentioned that on a nationwide basis, 6 percent of all institutional slots (in fiscal year 1972) were for LPN.

(2) In the sample areas there was very little institutional training in the following occupations with high demand ratings: LPN, building maintenance, electricity and electronics occupations, carpenter, assembler, sales clerk, upholsterer, and heating, cooling, and air conditioning occupations.

(3) There was *no* institutional training in the following high-demand occupations: bookkeeping and accounting, keypunch operator,[5] shipping and receiving occupations, wholesale sales occupations, electrician, bricklayer, plumber, transportation occupations, sheet metal worker, and roofer.

(4) There was heavy MDTA institutional training in the following medium demand occupations: nurse's aide, food preparation, metal machine occupations, and auto body repair.

If we eliminate the above occupations which, for one reason or another, are not suitable for MDTA institutional training, only four groups of occupations with substantial skill content in which there is little or no MDTA training are left: electricity and electronics occupations, bookkeeping and accounting occupations, keypunch operator (see footnote 5), and wholesale sales occupations. To these, segments of the heating, cooling, and air conditioning cluster and LPN could be added in some areas. Nevertheless, the fact remains that MDTA planners persist in the traditional occupations because those are the areas in which they have had the greatest placement success. There is no evidence that shifting to the unexploited occupational groups would increase program success.

## National Shortage Occupations

Four clusters of occupations have been declared "national shortages": medical (or health), environmental, law enforcement occupations, and construction trades. Experience with them is of particular interest.

---

[5] On a national level, in fiscal year 1971, a total of 1,311 persons were enrolled in keypunch operator and related data processing occupations.

### Medical (or Health)

Nearly 10 percent of all institutional slots were in the medical or health occupations cluster. Moreover, the range of occupations within the cluster was quite wide. The health occupations cluster, excluding LPN and the nurse refresher course, had the highest placement rate of any institutional program and even more surprising, was serving the most disadvantaged clientele. LPN and nurse refresher courses which served the least disadvantaged clientele had the second highest performance rating.

### Environmental, Law Enforcement, and Construction Trades

Four cities allocated a total of 208 slots to environmental occupations; three cities allocated a total of 90 slots to the construction trades; only 20 slots in one city had been allocated to law enforcement. (On a national basis, however, the "protection service" training being given through Project Transition is significant in the law enforcement field). It is too early to assess the effectiveness of these courses, although preliminary returns show that initial placement rates were high, but after six months few enrollees in these courses remained in training-related jobs.

### Major Inhibitors

There are six inhibitors of MDTA training in demanded occupations: (1) short length of training, coupled with emphasis on serving the disadvantaged, (2) the lack of a system for collecting, synthesizing, and storing occupational information at the local level, (3) the scarcity of funds, (4) union opposition in some occupational areas, (5) the tendency of newly created MDTA institutions to move toward a "stable" situation, and (6) employer hiring practices. Only the first three appear to have a significant effect.

### Length of Training

Faced with limited funds far exceeded by program eligibility, administrators have preferred a lean program for maximum enrollment to a rich program for a few. The number of occupations in which disadvantaged people can be trained to even entry levels in an average of 29 weeks is limited. There is no evidence that replacement of the present training occupations by others accessible within the 29-week average would improve results. There is reason to believe that expanding to a full 104 weeks would not only improve results by making accessible new and higher skilled occupations, it is also likely that a longer training period would multiply success in some of the current training offerings.

### Lack of Occupational Information

The almost total lack of a system to provide planners with synthesized, easy to understand, demand information *at the local level* may be the most significant of the six major inhibitors. Lacking information, administrators are more likely to stay within the relatively narrow range of occupational offerings which have been shown to produce reasonable success in institutional manpower training programs.

### Scarcity of Funds

MDTA allocations are inadequate to meet the needs for training in any given city or area. The question therefore is not one of broadening an existing program but it is one of selecting which occupations are the most suitable for a limited program. There is a natural reluctance to drop existing courses because to do so necessitates the purchase of new equipment and curricula materials, thereby decreasing the portion of funds available for actual training.

### Union Opposition

Union opposition, or what MDTA planners assume to be union opposition, occurs mainly in the construction and printing trades and in sewing occupations. A few breakthroughs have been made in the first two areas, but for the most part, both are considered "untouchable" by MDTA planners at the local and state levels. Sewing occupations continue to be "bootlegged," but are generally unattractive jobs. Ruling out occupations for union opposition results in a 12 percent reduction in the potential MDTA "world."

### Need for Stability

Newly created MDTA institutions, such as Skills Centers and large multi-occupational centers, are not exempt from the institutional tendency to strive toward "stability." If a Skills Center's offerings were to change every year, the Skills Center would be in a perpetual state of turmoil. Skills Centers have no objections to *broadening* their occupational offerings (provided that adequate funds are available), but understandably, they *do* resist changes in existing occupational offerings.

### Employer Hiring Practices

It is impossible to document the extent to which employer hiring practices limit the occupational range of MDTA training. It is obvious that civil service regulations constitute a formidable barrier in the public sector, but in the private sector, there are few *formal* or written screening mechanisms which work against MDTA trainees. There were indicators that in a loose labor market, the lack of a high school diploma was used by employers to screen out applicants, and in many of the survey areas, ES personnel, union officials, and even some employers were frank to say that black applicants could not be hired in certain occupations.

### Employer Attitudes

A total of 25 to 30 employer interviews per city does not constitute a statistically sound measurement of employer opinion and practice. Nevertheless, some useful insights were provided.

Generally speaking, employers were uninformed, unenthusiastic, and disinterested in MDTA institutional training. Although there were regional differences, employers had little invited or self-initiated contact with the planners and operators of institutional training. Few knew which institutions were participating in MDTA or which occupations were included in the programs. Employers, virtually without exception, shared a stereotyped image of a public training program that was wasteful, overadministered, overstaffed, and generally ill equipped to deal with community manpower problems. *Few employers, however, could justify this image or document their charges, and very often they contradicted themselves.* For example, while condemning the overall program in strong terms, employers rated most MDTA graduates "average or better than average employees," and rated 70 percent as having average or better than average promotion potential.

This negative attitude may indicate that "horror" stories received more attention than "success" stories, but it may also be attributable to the relatively depressed economic conditions existing at the time of the survey. Most firms have not experienced manpower shortages over the past three years, and in fact, have been overwhelmed by the constant pressure of new applicants and referrals. In such a setting, employers are not apt to be open minded about public training programs.

Most employers, especially those who hire large numbers of semi-skilled workers, prefer OJT (their own as opposed to public OJT programs) over institutional training. Craft employers, for the most part, do not believe that institutional programs are producing workers with skills adequate to compete in the craft market. The basis of this criticism may be the relatively short length of most institutional programs. However, employer preference for OJT is based upon the employers' contention that it does not take six months to train, for example, a machine operator. Many employers maintain that they could do the job in two weeks *if they had a properly motivated individual.*

Other highlights from the employer interviews were as follows:

(1) More than 60 percent of all hires were direct transactions between employers and applicants.

(2) The most common adjustment to a skills shortage was to work employees overtime.

(3) No real breakthrough had been made in the area of public employment. Civil service regulations are still a major barrier to MDTA enrollees.

(4) Employer screening devices generally consist of a check of the prospective employee's application form and a person-to-person interview. Although education credentials are not a *formal* criterion, the lack of a high school diploma works against applicants in a loose labor market.

## The Record

ORC examined the characteristics of enrollees and performance records of individual projects by city and by occupational cluster. The purposes were to determine the extent to which MDTA institutional training is serving the disadvantaged, to find out in which occupations the nondisadvantaged are being trained, and to determine whether performance records provide clues as to which institutional offerings are in demand occupations. Two important observations emerged from this analysis:

(1) MDTA planners remain with the traditional occupations because it is in these areas that they have their greatest success.

(2) There is no policy (official or unofficial) of allocating some funds for the disadvantaged and some for filling skills shortage occupations.

More than 72 percent of all MDTA institutional slots in the 14 cities are in the following occupations: clerical, welding, automotive, health occupations, and the metal machine trades. These are the areas where MDTA training has been most successful.

Although there are some occupational areas which enroll mainly nondisadvantaged enrollees — LPN/RN and environmental occupations, for example — the vast majority of trainees are *not* assigned to occupational clusters according to their disadvantaged or nondisadvantaged status. In other words, MDTA planners at the state and local levels do not interpret the 65 percent guideline to mean that 35 percent of all institutional slots should be reserved for the nondisadvantaged in *different occupational areas* (skills shortage areas, for example). On the contrary, the disadvantaged and nondisadvantaged are assigned, with few exceptions, to the same occupational clusters.

## Summary

The MDTA coordinator in one of the areas visited by ORC had a sign in his office which he said was illustrative of his confusion: I feel more like I do now than when I came in. He went on to say that "planning" for manpower does not exist. There is no information upon which local decisions can be based, and even if there were, it is doubtful if the regional and national offices of DOL would allow local decisions to stand. Allocations for manpower funds are made at the national level; information concerning these allocations usually arrives at the state and local levels too late to permit planning in any real sense. Furthermore, once allocations have been made, they are "locked in." If a local planner could prove that the mix of work experience, OJT, and institutional training was wrong for his area, he would be unsuccessful in his attempts to change that mix.

As the administration of manpower programs becomes more decentralized, this situation may change. It is becoming increasingly obvious that solutions to manpower problems must be found at the labor market level, identifying the problems that exist, setting objectives, devising solutions tailored to the needs of the local labor markets, garnering resources from wherever they can be obtained; then monitoring, evaluating, and modifying the emerging programs to bring them to success. Labor markets are local, regional, national, and even international in scope, but for most labor market transactions, it is the geographical scope within which the worker can commute to his daily job that is relevant.

Generally speaking, MDTA is training in demand occupations, but 73 percent of all MDTA training is in only five occupational clusters: clerical, automotive, health occupations, welding, and metal machine trades. These, with the possible exception of some health and clerical occupations, are traditional vocational education occupational offerings. In fact, vocational education was severely criticized in the late 1950s and early 1960s for training exclusively in these and a few other so-called "declining" occupations. MDTA is experimenting with some nontraditional occupations, but in most cases, these programs are dropped because of poor performance results. One of the primary reasons for their failure appears to be lack of knowledge of the kind of training required to assure success.

If decentralization is to be a success, an improved system must be installed from the local level up for identifying the *total* universe of need, the kinds of services required by subgroups within that universe of need, and for collecting, synthesizing, storing, and disseminating labor market information — in a usable form — for a variety of users.

At the present time, no system exists for defining or identifying skills shortage occupations at the local level, despite the introduction of computerized data gathering systems, the existence of a national industrial matrix, the methodologies for forecasting national occupational needs, applicant information (including unemployment insurance transactions), and other valid sources of information. No system exists for synthesizing and storing occupational information emanating from many sources. For the most part, the research and statistics staffs of ES are operating as field staffs to generate aggregate data that are used in identifying national or state trends; they are not providing staff services to the operating arms of ES. As a result, planning is left to those least capable of understanding complicated information-gathering systems and methodologies for identifying demand or skills shortage occupations, or for making occupational forecasts.

If information that is generated by Job Bank, ESARS, and JOLT could be adapted for local use and staff could be trained in how to apply national matrices and methodologies to local areas, the situation would be much improved. At the present time, the computerized systems, if used at all, are used to evaluate local office performance rather than to help improve performance or to gain insights into the occupational needs of communities.

This issue goes beyond skills shortages . . . it questions whether the entire field of occupational information is adequate at local or regional levels — adequate not just for MDTA institutional training but for vocational education, junior and community colleges, the job-seeking public, and brokers (interviewers, counselors, job developers, placement officers, etc.) who are charged with the public function of helping the jobless find employment. When considered in this light, the absence of usable occupational data at the local level is very serious indeed.

# 5

# Contributions of MDTA to Training Policy

Ten years' experience under MDTA cannot answer all of the questions relative to the stance public policy should take toward skills training. It is a remedial training effort directed primarily toward those who are already in the labor market and in trouble there. It has been separated from and rarely integrated with preparatory training for those yet to enter the labor market or with upgrading those who are already successful but who have ambitions for greater success. But the MDTA experience should be able to say some useful things about remedial adult occupational preparation, a task unlikely to wither away, even with the best initial preparation.

Financial encouragement to employers to train on the job those eligible for MDTA did not include public involvement in the content of training. Little has been learned from MDTA-OJT except which persons employers are willing to accept under what conditions, and what happens to their employment stability and earnings. What can be contributed here, after a summary of the findings of the studies reviewed in earlier chapters, is some insight into the role of institutional training as a remedial component for those finding it difficult to compete successfully for available jobs.

## SUMMARY OF CONCLUSIONS

The single most important fact emerging from the tenth year evaluation of MDTA is that on the best evidence available, the average institutional enrollee had increased earnings because of his enrollment of $1,250 per year. The gain for the average OJT enrollee was $1,100. Lack of an acceptable control group leaves the conclusion challengeable, but no more so than the various control groups which have been proposed for manpower evaluations. Every reasonable contingency has been accounted for, and the conclusion for the 1969 enrollees is the most reasonable possible. Whether that gain makes the program worth its costs rests upon a value judgment and an issue which only the future could decide: (1) Is it legitimate to spend public funds to increase the earnings of this particular universe of people? (2) Will the earnings gains estimated for the first year after training persist for as long as two years? If the answer to both is yes, the effort was worthwhile. If the answer to either is no, the program, at least for that body of enrollees, was a mistake. Since the enrollees were those designated by the Congress, the program successfully passes the first test. The limited longitudinal evidence available (cited in chapter 2) indicates an endurance of some earning differential over a control group for at least five years.

Underlying the annual earnings gains, it is significant that disadvantaged workers appear to have profited more than those not so disadvantaged, that completers profited more than noncompleters, and that longer training was more effective than shorter training. It is noteworthy that gains came by offering a new route to labor market entry or reentry, as well as from steadier employment and higher wages. Given the charge that manpower programs more often recycle disadvantaged workers through a secondary labor market rather than providing breakthroughs into a primary market, it is also significant that posttraining jobs were far more likely than pretraining jobs to provide the fringe benefits and job securities characteristic of the latter markets.

Beyond earnings gains were the contributions of institutional change. Class-size, remedial, institutional training projects were an innovation, but they limited the range of occupational choice and provided few supportive services. The Skills Center with its more specific adaptations to the needs of the disadvantaged was a more promising development. Skills Centers did not invent on-site counseling, cluster training, and open-entry/open-exit individualized instruction and basic education linked to skills training, but they enhanced the development of these concepts and broadened their exposure within vocational training. Individual referrals are also a useful development, supporting the possibilities of voucher systems for the retraining and upgrading of adults needing financial support to make such advancement possible.

It is difficult to isolate the impact of manpower experience upon vocational-technical education, but it is undoubtedly significant. The emergence of a National Manpower Training Association as a constituent group within the American Vocational Association enhances that influence, as well as giving manpower program staff vestiges of professionalization. Area Manpower Institutes for the Development of Staff (AMIDS) sponsored by the Division of Manpower Development and Training in the U.S. Office of Education and supported from MDTA funds, represent the only significant federal effort to provide in-service training for manpower program staffs. A current evaluation may provide a measure of that contribution.

The Skills Centers, like other aspects of the manpower programs which have specialized in service to the disadvantaged and to minorities, have contributed significantly to the development of a minority civil service. They have provided an entry route into professional and paraprofessional occupations for many who would have been unlikely to find them elsewhere. The MDTA program can also be credited with creation of new paraprofessional occupations. This is particularly true of the LPN, created despite the criticism of professional nurses associations to fill the space between the registered nurse and the nurse's aide.

Though it has not been a subject of this study, note should be taken of the contributions of the research and experimental aspects of Title I of MDTA. The researchers attracted to the study of labor markets, the expansion of knowledge concerning labor market institutions and their pathologies, the experimentation with the techniques to aid special groups (youth, women, minorities, rural and urban residents, the physically, mentally, the emotionally handicapped, prisoners and released offenders), and the spreading awareness of the importance of manpower and employment issues through dissemination of the results of research and through the Manpower Report of the President have and will have long-range impacts worth far more than their modest costs.

Those are the positive contributions, some measurable, and others not. Weaknesses of the program are also numerous, but they only reduce its effectiveness. There is no reason to attribute to them absolute harm.

One weakness is in the eye of the beholder, not in the program. Those who criticize training programs for not reducing unemployment are simply unrealistic. Training prepares people to fill jobs, it does not create jobs (except for the staffs who man the programs). If there were significant labor shortages in occupations within reach of the program, job vacancies could be reduced, but there are none in appreciable numbers. An effective training program might improve the labor force and facilitate matching supply and demand sufficiently to allow aggregate economic growth policies to accelerate job creation with lessened inflationary consequences. But that is only speculation. Training has not been sufficiently widespread to provide a test. Neither can training solve nonlabor market problems — alcoholism, drug addiction, crime, dependence of families without a potentially employable wage earner — though it can often supplement more direct solutions.

To some extent, criticism of MDTA for failure to reduce unemployment is just retribution for unrealistic promises of some of the program's architects. Even with the high unemployment of 1961–62, many were concerned that jobs were going begging for technologically displaced "square pegs" who could be changed by retraining to fit the available "round holes." Evidently, many politicians still harbor these unrealistic expectations and judge training programs by them. Manpower or any other public program must be evaluated by the extent to which it accomplishes what it can reasonably be expected to accomplish and by the usefulness of those possibilities, not by the overpromises of past publicists.

Remedial skills training and its accompanying supportive services must be justified by either (1) facilitating simultaneous job creation policies which open new opportunities for the trainees or (2) enabling the disadvantaged to compete successfully for jobs already available, regardless of the impact upon those who would have otherwise obtained the jobs. Equalizing opportunity is a goal which requires no apology. It is in essence among the long-term goals of the American society, even though it is always a cost to those who have previously been able to monopolize opportunity.

Broadening the franchise reduces the impact of every individual vote. Encouraging entrepreneurship increases competition for existing businesses. Collective bargaining may be fostered at the expense of employer profits. Free public education reduces the competitive advantage which might have been enjoyed by those who would have purchased their own education. Public policy should seek to expand the total supply of opportunity but cannot neglect its distribution. However, training without a clear connection to available jobs can be another frustrating failure experience for those who intuitively measure the equality of their opportunities by the equality of the results.

The most serious weakness of the MDTA program has been the occupations in which it has chosen to train. They are understandable as an expedient choice for "reasonable expectation of employment." Had the objective been a satisfactory working career for the remainder of each enrollee's working life, the choices would have been generally different.

Though it was never an intention of the legislation, MDTA has provided in too many places a second-class training institution for those least able to bear further stigmatization. Using substandard facilities and allowing equipment to deteriorate and become obsolete may save budgets, but the evidence is that it reduces the benefits at least as much as the costs.

Individual referral offers a standard training environment because it includes MDTA trainees in regular courses. But it provides no supportive services and therefore is useful only for those who needed no more than a stipend to make training possible and attractive. Skills Centers provide the supportive services; but they not only suffer from substandard facilities, they are also segregated institutions demarcated "for the disadvantaged only."

None of these weaknesses has been sufficient to offset the program's benefits, but they have undoubtedly reduced the payoff. The issues for the future are how the present program can be improved and what the experience can contribute to a sound remedial training component within national manpower policy.

## Toward a Training Policy for the United States

From ten years of experience with MDTA, it should be possible to do more than draw lessons for the improvement of the program itself. For the first time, the United States has had a national training policy for adults, if only for a limited group of people under specified circumstances. The nearest to such a policy prior to MDTA was the national funding for vocational education. At the time of MDTA's passage and before the Vocational Education Act of 1963, that policy was to spend small sums of federal money to entice states to match them to support training in occupational areas specified by federal law. The 1963 Act shifted emphasis from the skill needs of the labor market to the employment needs of workers and began acceleration of federal expenditures on vocational education. However, there was no policy for adult vocational education. States could choose at their own discretion to allocate some of the vocational education dollars made available to them to adults at the expense of youth.

There grew up three levels of vocational education: secondary, postsecondary, and adult. The first two were for full-time student youth; the latter part time for employed adults seeking to upgrade their skills. There were no provisions for full-time training of unemployed or out of the labor force adults unless they could enroll as regular students and had their own means of financial support. Even if they had earned unemployment compensation benefits, trainees or students were interpreted to be unavailable for work and therefore ineligible to draw upon that means for support during training. Adult education, as contrasted to adult vocational education, was overwhelmingly avocational.

Since MDTA's original target group was experienced adult workers of long labor force attachment, its essence was the substitution of training allowances for unemployment insurance, thus removing a disincentive to a full-time effort to upgrade and develop new skills. As the emphasis shifted to the disadvantaged, the genealogy was extended but not basically changed. MDTA was now a remedial adult vocational education program, most of the recipients of which were not eligible for unemployment compensation but probably had an even greater need for income support.

To isolate MDTA's lessons for a training policy, it is necessary to perceive it in this role of remedial adult vocational education, differing from other adult vocational education primarily in three ways:

(1) Full rather than part time

(2) Stipend for income support

(3) The need for job placement as early as possible to reinstitute basic family income

Few if any would advocate adult education as a device for reducing general levels of unemployment. Only if there were unfillable job vacancies for which training could prepare people, could there be a significant effect of training upon unemployment rates. Yet many — policymakers, as well as practitioners — have come to expect MDTA as a new remedial training component of adult education to do what adult education was never designed or able to do.

## Who Is to Be Served and How?

Evidence is ample that the average enrollee in an MDTA training program profited sufficiently to make the effort and expense worthwhile. It is also clear that far more people are in need of and could profit from remedial training than can be accommodated by present programs. The issue for manpower development and training is not whether it has been worthwhile; it is how it can be made more useful. Those who profited from training might have profited even more from some other manpower service. There may have been others more in need of training than those who received it. Training for other occupations or with different techniques or better administration might have increased the payoff. Thus the most critical issue for a remedial training program is *who can profit most from what kind of training under which conditions.*

The advantaged versus the disadvantaged argument as it is usually formulated is of no assistance in answering the "who" issue. The definition of disadvantaged was construed as an evaluative instrument rather than as an aid to management decisions. The directive to favor those variously disadvantaged in the competition for jobs had been issued, but there was no measure to determine when a project had complied. The categories chosen were those among whom unemployment and low incomes were known to be concentrated. But the categories themselves are not evidence or explanation of an individual's state of being disadvantaged. One is not unemployed because he is young but because youth tend to be inexperienced or excessively mobile, or because employers discriminate because of age. Being over 45 years old, without a high school education, or being a member of a minority group may be a surrogate for lack of substantive knowledge, a limited number of remaining working years, or employer discrimination. Of the disadvantaged criteria, only physical or mental handicap is likely to represent a real obstacle to productivity, and that only for certain handicaps and certain jobs. The problem is to identify those for whom the real ob-stacles to adequate employment and income are such that they can be removed by a training program.

Several criteria suggest themselves. The trainee must be an in-dividual who has a reasonable chance of profiting more from the pro-gram than he would from simply receiving the equivalent of the training cost as a simple one-time transfer payment. That is, training may be use-ful therapy for an alcoholic or a drug addict, but there should be a specific decision based on evidence or judgment of success. Similarly, training for a welfare mother should follow a decision that employment following training is a realistic objective or that the general upgrading of skills and education will be useful sans a job. Training for an in-dividual should only follow a decision that an equal or better job was not likely without the training or through some alternative, less expen-sive remedial activity. There should also be a judgment either that em-ployment would be made more likely following training or that the individual's long-term employment and earnings prospects would be enhanced while not costing excessively in foregone current earnings.

Obviously, these criteria are based on judgments concerning in-dividuals and their prospects. These are not decisions which can be made in a rule book and handed down from higher levels. The criteria argue for establishing general guidelines and training local staff to make appropriate decisions without undue pressure to fill slots. The criteria also argue for continuous evaluation and assessment at a project level to determine who is profiting and who is not, and which program com-ponents are and are not contributing.

Conceptually, if it can be applied, the greatest need is a shift in objectives from immediate employment to a successful remaining work-ing career. The reasonable expectation of employment criteria and assessment by placement rate have together been responsible for an unduly short-run focus. Trainees with family responsibilities do need a return to employment as rapidly as possible, but that does not prevent viewing that employment in a longer run career context. Younger enrollees are not usually under such stringent financial pressures. As a permanent remedial and occupational component of adult education, concepts currently described as career education[1] are applicable to

---

[1] Kenneth B. Hoyt et al., Career Education: What It Is and How to Do It (Salt Lake City: Olympus Publishing Company, 1972).

MDTA practices. The individual's age, sex, family status and related factors determine the number of years left in the labor market. As difficult as foresight is, the program objective should be an employability plan for each individual based on remaining working life and realistic opportunity. The relative seriousness of lack of skill as an obstacle to employment is more readily apparent in that career focus. Good mental and physical health, human relations skills, basic education, and knowledge of the labor market are examples of attributes necessary to successful work life. Remediation of those deficiencies may be more difficult but no less possible than remediation of skill deficiencies.

## Training in a Decategorized Manpower Program

This individualized approach also requires flexibility, discretion, and decategorization in manpower programs. A one-to-one relationship of client and counselor exists in a number of programs. The missing element is access to a full array of services so that a package of them can be tailored to individual needs. Such flexibility has been advocated throughout the decade. It has often been promised but never delivered. The WIN employability teams were an example. They had the assignment to review client needs but confronted the most difficult of all clientele with limited service availability.

The decentralization and decategorization advocated in various comprehensive manpower bills have had as their primary motive the ability to adapt services to individual and local needs. Actually, the two terms obfuscate more than they clarify. The issue is manpower planning at the labor market and individual level. Many MDTA administrators oppose the comprehensive bills, fearing both the uncertainties of new administrative relationships and a possible reduction in the total amount of institutional training. DOL's lack of enthusiasm for institutional training is the major source of those fears. However, Congress has been willing to write into legislation a role guarantee for HEW and the education hierarchy at the state level.

A sensible approach would be to merge the entire education and manpower function into a human resource department at the federal level. Nevertheless, it is unlikely that state or local manpower planners would overlook or downgrade the training function. They are in a better position than national planners to identify training needs, education generally has greater political clout at the state and local levels than at the national level, and there are so few effective manpower tools available that planners and implementers of plans are likely to opt for training by default. Whereas DOL dominance in manpower policy at the national level may tend toward lessened training, education influence at the state and local levels is at least as likely to imply an overemphasis on institutional training.

At any rate, labor market planning, including the training function, requires a labor market information system, ongoing research into the universe of need and the nature of the client groups, comprehension of all relevant manpower and education services and budgets, skillful planning staff, the discretion to plan, and the clout to see plans implemented.

A stronger role for educators in labor market manpower planning might be a useful antidote to the present excessive focus on immediate placement in high-turnover jobs. The risk is to overemphasize training in contrast to alternative manpower services. Nevertheless, the most vitally needed reform in manpower training is to open up more substantial occupations in which enrollees may reasonably expect to launch a lasting new career. There is no guarantee that using the full 104 weeks of MDTA authorization would not simply result in a higher dropout rate, but experimentation with that possibility is long overdue.

*Training Allowances*

The considerations discussed above come full circle to the "who to serve" issue. There are those who can and would stand still long enough to profit from a two-year training course and those who for reasons of economics or personality require the shortest possible route to a job. The level of stipends is an important consideration. Stipends should be high enough to enable those who can profit from any particular length of training to continue in it, yet not so high as to encourage individuals to enroll for the stipend alone. The coupling of income maintenance with manpower services has an adverse effect on both programs, but without a general availability of income support, there is little choice. The early Opportunities Industrialization Center (OIC) program, a self-help program created by blacks mainly for blacks, rejected the idea of allowances. OIC's founder, the Reverend Leon Sullivan, contended that enrollees in training programs must be motivated to master the training offered if such programs are to be truly effective. The payment of allowances, he maintained, has a tendency to vitiate that kind of motivation.

Enrollees who enter the program mainly for allowances are apt to drop out whenever their need for supplementary income is eliminated (if they find a job, for example) and create problems for both instructors and other enrollees because of their lack of interest in the training itself. OIC eventually had to change its policy regarding the payment of allowances because it could not compete with federal programs which offered allowances together with training. Applicants who were offered two programs — one with and one without allowances — were apt to choose the program with allowances. The payment of allowances also makes it difficult for selection and referral personnel to fill slots with individuals who are really interested in obtaining skills training. The result is that very often applicants who are attracted primarily by allowances are selected over applicants who truly want to receive skills training.

Until there is some national policy on income maintenance, it will probably be necessary to couple training programs to such maintenance. But the implications of this kind of policy should be understood, and in the long run, policy consideration should be given to separating income maintenance from manpower training.

Ideally, the income maintenance issue could be met with the guaranteed income proposed as a welfare reform. If every family had a guaranteed basic income, plus the encouragement of a negative income tax system to earn more, the "program hustler" would have no encouragement to enroll. No stipend would be necessary. One would enroll only in response to long-term prospects for gain rather than responding to the availability of a training stipend.

Separation of training stipends from income maintenance has other unfortunate effects. As noted, MDTA training allowances were originally introduced as a substitute for unemployment compensation because trainees were ruled not available for work and therefore not eligible for unemployment compensation (which they could draw if they refrained from training). This factor remains the case in many states, and there is a tendency to draw unemployment compensation until earned benefits are exhausted before seeking a training program with its stipend. How much better it would be if unemployed workers without immediate prospects of being recalled to a job could use their compensated unemployment to refurbish and upgrade their skills.

*Training Institutions*

Labor market planners and administrators are in the best position to fit the type of training program to individual needs. The individual referral program appears to be the best device for training those without special need for supportive services. The attraction is not the low costs. Those are illusory. When public schools fail to charge the full cost of MDTA training, they are merely shifting the incidence of, not reducing the costs. Nor is the attraction better facilities. The practice of the worst facilities for those most in need of remedial training must be reversed.

The real attraction is integration into the mainstream of education and training and the avoidance of stigmatization, whether as perceived by others or by the trainee himself. The individual referral approach could have both the advantages and weaknesses of a voucher system. Decisions of where and in what to train are currently made by ES. Given good counseling and some review and approval of competent training institutions, the potential enrollee may be just as capable of wise choice. At least it should be tried.

As in any voucher approach, there will be the tendency for schools to recruit the easiest to train. However, this can be offset by a voucher of differential value, depending upon the relative state of the client's being disadvantaged. Veterans eligible for GI Bill benefits have been allowed to develop and choose their own readiness programs. There is no reason to suppose that the unemployed in general could not make wise choices if they were aided by knowledgeable and sympathetic counselors.

However, adequate service to the seriously disadvantaged will probably require continuing national support of a series of institutions with prescribed capabilities. The Skills Centers have met that need well, except for their tendency to train in poor facilities and their propensity toward socioeconomic segregation. However, the pattern for avoiding these evils already exists with the integration of Skills Centers into community colleges. A separate administrative unit within the school has responsibility for the welfare of MDTA enrollees. Yet the classes they enter are largely regular courses within the college. They are in no way identified to their fellow students as different. They receive college credit, and some have opted to continue beyond their MDTA entitlement to receive an associate degree. These are certainly appropriate sites for experimentation with the 104-week authorization. Both an obstacle and an advantage is the fact that the college which encompasses a Skills Center must reform itself to offer open-entry/open-exit, cluster training, supportive services, and other adaptations for all students in order to serve the manpower program clientele without identifying and stigmatizing them.

A voucher approach wherein a trainee could choose his own training programs and schools which would require certain minimum standards to be eligible could spark and accelerate institutional change. Admittedly, improving the quality of remedial training will increase costs and reduce the enrollments possible within limited budgets. But it is at least worth an experiment to see whether a richer program for fewer will not surpass in payoff a lean program for many.

*Manpower Planning and Decentralization*

A final element advocating labor market planning as the primary decision-making step in manpower training is the possibility of linking training to local economic conditions. Most labor markets at any point in time will reflect national economic conditions, but all will not. Many alternatives are conceivable. Some would argue for OJT in labor-short times to bring enrollees directly into employment, with institutional training advocated for slack times when unemployed people could upgrade their skills without foregoing current income. Others would argue against OJT in labor-short times when employers should be willing to train at their own expense and would prefer institutional training to bring the competitively disadvantaged to an entry level. Others might argue to train in expanding economies and spend all manpower funds on public service employment and other job creation efforts in slack markets. But the chances of coming up with the right answer are best when well-trained local labor market planners adapt to local need under the goad of monitoring and evaluating from the federal level.

Despite the advantages of local labor market planning to make manpower programs more responsive to needs at the local and state levels, several issues must be resolved if decentralization is to be effective. In the past, local and state political leaders have been in the envious position of claiming credit for manpower, model cities, and poverty grants, while at the same time disclaiming any responsibility for program performance. One congressman, when informed by one of the authors of this book that the city he represented was to be the recipient of $5 million CEP grant, put it this way: "This is the kind of program I like. I get the credit for bringing the money into the city, but when the program fails, the 'feds' get the blame."

The manpower revenue-sharing approach to decentralization has the promise of allowing the "feds" to disclaim any responsibility for program results. These individuals are in effect saying, "*We* will take the credit for making the grants, *you* accept the responsibility for program performance." States and local communities would receive federal grants with no strings attached. When and if decentralization becomes a reality, responsibility for failure will shift to state and local officials. Whether state and local political leaders will be willing to "pick up the ball" will depend to a great extent upon whether they view active participation as a political asset or liability. If they view manpower programs as an "albatross" around their necks, they will seek (and find) ways of dissociating themselves from program administration. It is doubtful that this kind of decentralization will result in any significant improvements.

There are legitimate roles for all three levels of government. State and local governments should have maximum flexibility in determining needs, the appropriate program mixes to serve those needs, and the evaluation of program results. The federal government, on the other hand, should assume responsibility for the following:

(1) Articulating the purposes of manpower programs, including their limitations, so that state and local administrators will not be expected to accomplish the impossible. This means accepting the proposition that most manpower programs affect only the supply side of the market, not the demand or jobs side.

(2) Seeing to it that manpower programs, as administered by state and local officials, do not operate counter to national goals or objectives. If for example it is a national objective to encourage the integration of Skills Centers with existing post-secondary vocational education institutions, the federal government should require state and local administrators to show evidence that they are indeed attempting to accomplish this. With regard to priorities, the federal government ought to reserve for itself the option of establishing priorities regarding return-

ing veterans, workers displaced because of loss of government contracts, or any changes in emphasis which may occur as a result of the revision or redesign of programs.

(3) Helping to establish a system of operations research which will provide state and local planners with the kinds of information they need to assess the total universe of need, to assess program performance, and most important of all, to provide a comprehensive flow of labor market information — not just on a national basis, but on a *local* and state basis. This may involve a complete redesign of current information systems to satisfy local and state needs first. National projections could then be drawn from a more comprehensive base of local and state information.

With respect to manpower planning, the third item is the most important. There can be no manpower planning without both client and labor market information. Yet the skills shortage evaluation demonstrated that there is almost a complete lack of labor market information — for manpower planning purposes — at the local level. It demonstrated also that very little is known about the total universe of need, or what mix of programs would best serve that need, at either the local or the state level. Finally, there is no present system for program monitoring and evaluation. Since the vast majority of resources allocated for research are controlled by federal agencies, this responsibility cannot be assigned solely to state and local governments.

The federal responsibility is clear . . . either a reallocation of resources for management information systems to state and local governments, together with technical assistance, is called for or federal systems must be redesigned to meet state and local needs. Labor market information does not mean merely gross lists of job vacancies or occupational projections; the system must also produce on a state and local basis such variables as pay rates by industry, nature and size of fringe benefits, job security, opportunity for advancement, schedule of hours, working conditions, education requirements, skills necessary, experience necessary, physical requirements, certifications necessary, requirements for union membership, and normal routes of entry. Local planners must also have access to information from the sources of supply — educational and training institutions, apprenticeship, manpower programs, placement agencies, and so forth.

State and local planners should be able to determine program mixes (based on client needs), economic conditions and other factors; but unless there is an improvement in the kinds of information needed to make key decisions, decentralization by itself will not result in improved manpower planning.

### Institutional versus On-the-Job Training

The choice between institutional and OJT has been an issue throughout the life of MDTA. OJT is cheaper and is directly attached to a job but is limited by job availability, the employer's willingness to cooperate, and his selection or acceptance of trainees. Institutional training can be undertaken anytime for anyone in any occupation the administrator chooses, but at higher cost and no assurance of employment. As a training method, OJT is appropriate for occupations wherein the job content is such that the trainee can be almost immediately productive while learning or for occupations which cannot be synthesized in a school, classroom, shop, or laboratory, where there is little danger to persons or equipment from unskilled performance. Institutional training is more appropriate where the theoretical content is extensive, where substantial training must precede production, where OJT supervision is difficult, where safety is an important consideration, and where the work setting can be sufficiently synthesized to give some realism to the training.

The need for income, the distrust of institutions, and the need for assurance that a job will follow training make OJT appropriate for the disadvantaged. But this is just the group employers have been most reluctant to accept. It is also the group most likely to need basic education and other supportive services which are more easily supplied institutionally. The job attachment of OJT is often illusory, offering only an entry-level, unskilled or semiskilled job of high turnover. Nothing very dramatic can be suggested. Coupling a preliminary institutional period with OJT is an obvious solution but has been little used. Vocational educators have, of course, a preference for institutional training, and they have no input into OJT. Employment services generally find it more convenient to refer applicants to a school program than to persuade employers to undertake OJT. OJT training subsidies have been very low, but employers seem generally more willing to accept $650

($25 a week for 26 weeks) for employing a less disadvantaged unemployed person than $3,000 a person for a NAB-JOBS contract for disadvantaged only. Cooperative education experience of vocational educators could well be applied to the coupling of institutional and OJT for those occupations for which OJT is more appropriate. That may not increase the amount, but can increase the quality of coupling by supervising the linkage of the learnings from both phases.

Institutional training's primary jurisdiction can be identified best by our observing which occupations are most likely to involve training in vocational and technical schools in the normal, nonremedial practice. Little effort has been made to link institutional training with a job commitment. To do so would require some sort of quid pro quo for employers. Probably the most effective route would be to use public service employment provisions to guarantee a job for a transitional period for anyone who successfully completes a manpower training program. If public agencies were unable to place the graduate, they would be obligated to employ him until nonsubsidized placement was achieved.

*Patterns of Labor Market Success*

To synthesize an appropriate long-run approach to remedial adult vocational education, it is worth examining how the successful "make it" and how the situation of the unsuccessful can be restructured to make possible the same achievement. Perhaps too much emphasis on pathology has obscured the path that is followed with such economic rewards by most.

What do we know about the patterns of labor market experience typical of successful participants? In general, these individuals are born into stable family units in which the father, and often the mother as well, experiences reasonably steady employment. Work and self-sufficiency is an important part of the family's value system. The family also lives in a neighborhood where the majority share the same work values. The individual accepts the discipline of school attendance, learning the basic skills taught there, and graduates from high school. In his exposure to the community at large, he absorbs considerable knowledge about what people do for a living. However, his detailed knowledge is likely to be limited to the occupations of his parents, close relatives, neighbors, and those from whom he receives direct services. He generally has some work experience in part time and vacation jobs before leaving school.

The majority pursue no specialized skills training in high school and receive no post-secondary training. After leaving school, they experience a succession of jobs, most of which are obtained through informal channels of relatives and friends. A conscious occupational choice is rarely made. One of the informally obtained series of jobs turns out to be permanent and reasonably satisfactory in pay and working conditions.

Most of those who enter college follow a similar pattern, but the primary occupation which emerges is more likely to be white collar. The minority who obtain specific skills training in high school or beyond are likely to enter that occupation at an entry level. The college graduates divide between those who still must go through the trial-and-error job choice orifice and those who attain job skills and ambitions which they exercise in an entry-level job before and after graduation. Labor market intermediaries such as ESs and other placement agencies play an insignificant part for most.

Undoubtedly, the most serious obstacle confronting all of the disadvantaged (and the nondisadvantaged poor) is simply the lack of attractive employment opportunities. There is ample evidence that fluctuations in economic prosperity make little difference in isolated rural areas. In large central cities, employment opportunities grow and contract, but too few central city residents seem to have access to the predominantly white-collar jobs which dominate those labor markets. They have also been effectively blocked from many of the public sector jobs which offer a middle employment level. The remaining unstructured array of low-level jobs gives no premium to tenure and offers little incentive for stability and productivity.

For the young just entering the labor market, there is much that remedial manpower programs could do to effectively apply career education principles. Those whose family and community backgrounds have been strictured have explored only a limited job world. Broader realities must be opened to them and explored by them. However, reform of both the training and the hiring processes will be necessary to give them a broader reality to explore. Availability of a longer training duration, linked with various forms of guided work experience (along with civil service reform), is probably the most vital need.

Even the best of vocational education prepares only for entry-level jobs. College graduation rarely prepares an individual to become immediately productive. Nearly everyone learns his job on the job. For that reason, many employers prefer to simply rely on OJT. But they base it on selection processes which screen out those with substandard preparation. Some of the most successful of vocational education programs have been those called "cooperative education" which link classroom training with supervised job experience. Apprenticeship, where it is appropriately supervised to assure a well-rounded experience accompanied by related classroom training, has been traditionally effective.

*Implications for Various Groups*

All of this suggests that for the young, a program could be established, using MDTA funds to provide remedial education accompanied by classroom skills and integrated with OJT experience. Two years' enrollment in that combination should provide for most not only training, but transition into an attractive job. The training should also supply credentials which would allow the individual to build toward an academic degree if he is so inclined. Examples are now available in the few community colleges which have integrated MDTA Skills Centers into the facilities, administration, and curriculum. Actually, few jobs requiring less than a baccalaureate degree should be out of reach with such a training combination. An additional advantage of the community college-MDTA route is avoidance of the stigma which attaches to institutions limited to the disadvantaged, especially since these individuals are usually housed in substandard facilities.

Civil service reform is emphasized because jobs in this sector are increasing most rapidly in number and in pay in the very areas where populations most in need of employment assistance are located. There is also adequate documentation that many merit system selection requirements are unrelated to ability to perform the job. Overqualification may be as costly to the public through high turnover as underqualification has been through shoddy performance. Elimination of criteria unrelated to potential performance, knowledge of the opportunities, and guidance in negotiating the maze could open important new opportunities. New Careers has tried with some success, but the effort has not been sufficiently concerted. The Public Service Careers program lacks the needed incentives. The Public Employment Program has missed a great opportunity. Lesser governments needed the money and personnel, and the federal government was paying the bill. It could have required reform and a quota of previously excluded applicants, but the public agencies were left to their own selection decisions.

The congressional push to make welfare recipients work threatens to dwarf all other manpower programs. As a general principle, there is nothing wrong with welfare recipients paying their own way. However, Congress and the general public consistently and perversely refuse to recognize that the bulk of the welfare population is female heads of family and their children. Able-bodied, non-aged males on welfare are rare. Once these realities are recognized, most would probably agree that the mother of several preschool children is possibly better off being taught motherhood and homemaking as an occupation than being trained for a job which could never support the family without being subsidized. For those with none or few preschool children, welfare mothers, like a high proportion of nonwelfare female heads of family and wives, may prefer to and probably should work. But again, it must be recognized that any attractive job with hope of full self-support will require some combination of extensive training and aided access. In fact, decently paid female jobs uniformly require more preparation than male jobs. It is almost certain to be more expensive in budgetary terms to employ welfare recipients than to provide them with income maintenance. Who should work requires greater selectivity than is presently being ascertained.

Taking care of the youth and female heads of family would leave in the pool of those with employment handicaps a heterogeneous group differing little from the average of the labor force. Among them would be persons with health, psychological, or behavioral problems of various degrees of severity. There are those whose primary problem is displacement by economic or technological change at an age when adjustment is difficult. There are those whose sole obstacle is location or access to a job. There are also those trapped in unchallenging and low-paid jobs who cannot find a ladder to move up. Of course, some are just lazy — a form of sickness in a work-oriented society. For many, the need is more aggressive use of subsidized OJT. There is obvious need to clarify the relative advantages of institutional training and OJT and to disseminate guidelines for choice between them as effective training techniques. It should also be generally recognized that though OJT can exist by itself, institutional training for adults (and even for youth) without some direct tie to a definite employment opportunity is a high-risk operation. Either there must be an advance commitment for a job or a commitment from both schools and placement agencies to expend all needed energies to attain satisfactory placement. As noted, a public service employment guarantee would be an ideal vehicle for this purpose.

All of this, however, is necessary but only short run. The objectives of manpower policy and programs should be:

(1) Satisfying work lives for all people

(2) Efficient allocation of labor resources

Neither is satisfied merely by getting a worker into a job. The notion of career implies a sequence of generally improving work attachments. The individual must have the opportunity to progress within his existing employment, find new employment if the old disappears, and move to new opportunities and challenges if the old stultifies or dissatisfies. Two innovations are clearly needed for the entire work force: (1) a retraining or placement program for those who are displaced or dissatisfied with their current employment and (2) an upgrading program for those whose potential and ambition remain unrealized.

Some European nations consider worthwhile general educational and training programs for all workers to increase their productivity and job satisfactions.[2] They tend to use sheltered employment for the seriously disadvantaged and upgrading training for those of sound employability potential. A general worker self-renewal program financed from, or in ways similar to unemployment compensation trust funds has been proposed to train midcareer, midskill workers for jobs at higher skills.[3] Employed workers would move up the skill ladder a step at a time through periodic part-time or sabbatical training, opening up lower and middle level skills for the unskilled and disadvantaged. The alternatives are numerous, the costs not extreme, and the potential gains in labor force quality and personal welfare substantial. The possibility of lowering the unemployment-inflation cost trade-off is enticing. A general program of remedial occupational training is the clear implication of the MDTA experience.

---

[2] Beatrice Reubens, "Manpower Policy in Western Europe," *Manpower Magazine* (Nov. 1972).

[3] U.S. Department of Health, Education and Welfare, *Work in America*, report of a special task force to the Secretary of Health, Education and Welfare (Dec. 1972), pp. 103–08.

## Summary: The Role of Training in Manpower Policy

It has become popular to say with some pomposity about manpower policy, "We have concentrated on the supply side too much. Now we must direct our efforts to the demand side." A much better formulation would be, "The demand side is appropriate for short-run actions or for long-range economic development, but long-range manpower needs are more appropriately a task for supply efforts." Advocacy of more attention to the demand for labor in manpower policy rarely includes fiscal and monetary policies to increase purchasing power and the consequent aggregate demand for goods and services and for workers to produce them. It is generally recognized that the rate of job creation can be speeded up and unemployment can be reduced anytime we are willing to accept the inflationary consequences of doing so. Allusions to the demand side of manpower programs refer more often to specific job creation targeted for particular groups through:

(1) Work experience and training programs such as Neighborhood Youth Corps and Operation Mainstream

(2) Subsidized private employment such as MDTA-OJT or NAB-JOBS

(3) Public service employment

Short of identifying labor shortage occupations within the reach of manpower training programs, there is little that a remedial program can do to reduce general levels of unemployment in the short run. It can possibly improve the quality of the labor force and improve the match between demanded and supplied labor. Therefore the cost from inflation at any particular level of economic growth and job creation may be reduced, allowing more aggressive exercise of fiscal and monetary policies. But this is a long-run, not a short-run phenomenon.

Adult remedial occupational training should therefore be approached as a long-run strategy, both for the individual and the labor force. For the individual, the question should be: Given the number of years from now to retirement, what combination of manpower and supportive services and what preparation for what occupations are most likely to maximize the individual's income and satisfactions over the period? For the labor force, the query should be similar: What policies will maximize the productivity and adaptability of the labor force?

Since it is the first law of economics that there will never be enough resources to do all that society would like to do, the critical decision for manpower policy joins the individual and collective queries: What works best for whom under what circumstances?

The compelling evidence appears to be that the disadvantaged have profited more from manpower training than their nondisadvantaged counterparts, but the criteria of the disadvantaged are not designed to answer the question: Who needs what? Their purpose is evaluative. They measure whether a program or project is concentrating upon those groups who are most likely to be poor or unemployed. They do not identify the reasons for any particular person's straitened circumstances. Among those who meet the disadvantaged criteria are likely to be many who could profit from training and many who could not, some who could profit from some types of training but not from other types, and some who could profit a little and some a great deal. No measurable specified criteria can be placed in a manual to designate what kinds of people should and should not be trained. Only the broadest of criteria can be suggested to be applied on a case-by-case basis jointly by an individual and his counselor: (1) Can this individual profit more by training than by some alternative set of services or by simply being given the equivalent cost in a lump sum payment? (2) Is there any other person or group designated by society's values as more deserving of assistance?

MDTA has been worth the cost and effort. The weight of evidence supports its effectiveness as a device to increase the employment and earnings of its enrollees. It has contributed to the ability of vocational training institutions to serve the disadvantaged, and it has opened new occupations and avenues of employment to both trainees and staff. It needs a longer run focus on broader concepts of employability and more substantial occupations. It deserves and needs integration into more prestigious institutional settings, but with special care to see that the disadvantaged are served within those settings.

Individualized employability plans and local labor market planning with federal technical assistance, staff training, monitoring and evaluation could increase the appropriateness of the training. Improved labor market information will be necessary to that planning. A more effective training program without economic growth can equalize employment opportunity without expanding the supply of opportunity. But equalizing opportunity is a traditional and worthy goal.

Program improvement is a never-ending task. The important message is that the remedial training function within manpower programs needs improvement but that it has been and remains worthwhile.

# Bibliography

Borus, Michael E. "Time Trends in the Benefits from Retraining in Connecticut." *Twentieth Annual Winter Proceedings of the Industrial Relations Research Association, December 1967.* Madison: University of Wisconsin Press, 1968.

Decision Making Information. *MDTA Outcomes Study.* Final report no. CAL-7778, prepared for the U.S. Department of Labor, Manpower Administration, Office of Evaluation. Santa Ana: Decision Making Information, 1971.

Downs, Anthony. "Up and Down with Ecology: The Issue-Attention Cycle." *The Public Interest,* no. 28 (Summer 1972).

*Effectiveness of Manpower Training Programs: A Review of Research on the Impact on the Poor, The.* Paper no. 3 of *Studies in Public Welfare,* a staff study prepared for the Subcommittee on Fiscal Policy, Joint Economic Committee, 92d Congress. Washington, D.C.: U.S. Government Printing Office, November 20, 1972.

Gurin, Gerald. *A National Attitude Study of Trainees in MDTA Institutional Programs.* Ann Arbor: Survey Research Center, University of Michigan, August 1970.

Hardin, Einar, and Borus, Michael E. "Benefits and Costs of MDTA-ARA Retraining." *Industrial Relations* (May 1972).

Hoyt, Kenneth B., *et al. Career Education: What It Is and How to Do It.* Salt Lake City: Olympus Publishing Company, 1972.

Main, Earl D. "A Nationwide Evaluation of MDTA Institutional Job Training." *Journal of Human Resources* (Spring 1968).

Mangum, Garth L. *MDTA, Foundation of Federal Manpower Policy.* Baltimore: Johns Hopkins Press, 1968.

————, and Robson, R. Thayne, eds. *Metropolitan Impact of Manpower Programs: A Four-City Comparison.* Salt Lake City: Olympus Publishing Company, 1973.

Muir, Allan H., *et al. Cost Effectiveness Analysis of On-the-Job and Institutional Training Courses.* Washington, D.C.: Planning Research Corporation, 1967.

North American Rockwell Information Systems Company. *A Systems Analysis of the MDTA Institutional Training Program.* Final report. Washington, D.C.: North American Rockwell Information Systems Company, March 1971.

————. *MDTA Basic Education Program.* Preliminary report, 1972. (Book is currently in process.)

Olympus Research Corporation. *Evaluation of the Effectiveness of Institutional Manpower Training in Meeting Employers' Needs in Skills Shortage Occupations.* Final report. Salt Lake City: Olympus Research Corporation, June 1972.

————. *Evaluation of Manpower Development and Training: Skills Centers.* Final report. Salt Lake City: Olympus Research Corporation, February 15, 1971.

————. *Evaluation of the MDTA Institutional Individual Referral Program.* Final report. Salt Lake City: Olympus Research Corporation, June 1972.

Reubens, Beatrice. "Manpower Policy in Western Europe." *Manpower Magazine* (November 1972).

Sewell, David O. *Training the Poor.* Kingston, Ontario: Industrial Relations Center, Queen's University, 1971.

Somers, Gerald G., ed. *Retraining the Unemployed.* Madison: University of Wisconsin Press, 1968.

————, and McKechnie, Graehme H. "Vocational Retraining Programs for the Unemployed." *Twentieth Annual Winter Proceedings of the Industrial Relations Research Association, December 1967.* Madison: University of Wisconsin Press, 1968.

U.S. Office of Health, Education and Welfare. *Work in America.* Report of a special task force to the Secretary of Health, Education and Welfare, December 1972.

# Index

DATE DUE